Sedulo curavi humanas actiones non ridere, non lugere, neque detestari sed intelligere
　　　　　　　　　—SPINOZA.
　　　　　　　　　Tractatus Politicus.
　　　　　　　　　Cap. I. Sec. 4.

I have sedulously endeavored not to laugh at human actions, not to deplore them, nor to detest them, but merely to understand them.

OUR BATTLE

by

HENDRIK WILLEM VAN LOON

being one man's answer to

MY BATTLE

by

ADOLF HITLER

SIMON AND SCHUSTER

NEW YORK · 1938

SECOND PRINTING

 55

PRINTED IN THE UNITED STATES OF AMERICA
AMERICAN BOOK—STRATFORD PRESS, INC., NEW YORK

OUR BATTLE

OUR BATTLE

YESTERDAY, at a meeting in honor of the late Christopher Columbus (discoverer of the West Indies), the name of the Mayor of the greatest city in our western democracy was booed while the name of a foreign dictator was greeted with tumultuous applause.

This morning I went to New York. I expected to find the city in a turmoil of resentful excitement. I expected to see vigilantes patrolling the streets. I expected to see all good and trusted citizens rallying to the colors besmirched by the fact that the name of New York's Mayor had been hissed while the name of a foreign dictator had been wildly cheered. I expected at the very least to read editorials in all the papers, stating in terms of a most righteous indignation that such a state of affairs was simply not to be tolerated and that those who had booed the name of New York's duly elected chief executive, while the name of a foreign dictator (and an open and avowed enemy of all democratic forms of government) had been welcomed with enthusiastic approval. . . . I expected to hear from our national government that those pseudo citizens who were responsible for this outrage would at once be put on board ship and would be given free transportation to that country to which they had remained so pathetically loyal in spite of their oath of allegiance to the Constitution of the United States of America.

And what did I find?

A complete indifference! A most complete and abject indifference! At best, a mildly amused attitude which tried to laugh the whole matter off as a rather unfortunate joke. Some people said, "Oh well, the Little Flower has a sense of humor—he can take it." Others complacently shrugged their shoulders. "This is a free country," they casually remarked, "so what of it?"

Others again argued that all this was politics and what, with an election on our hands, could we expect? Still others had a personal grievance against the chief executive, who had made them pay more taxes than they liked, and were therefore quite willing to let him have a little of his own medicine. But no one (with very few exceptions) seemed to have been struck by the fact that that little incident went to the very roots of our national existence and that it was a symptom of decay which should fill our hearts with the most serious misgivings about the future of our own commonwealth. For the name of the duly elected chief magistrate of the greatest city of all modern democracies had been hooted, while the name of a foreign dictator and a sworn enemy of all democratic forms of government had been greeted with cheers of delight, and nothing had been done about it—nobody had protested—the whole matter had been accepted as an absurd but quite unimportant incident to be quickly forgotten without any further comment, for "Who in Hell cares?"

That is the reason I am writing this little book.

Who in Hell cares?

Well, I do!

When a nation loses its interest in its own destiny, then that nation is doomed. I do not want to see our nation doomed, for then the last hope of the world for a truly decent and human form of existence would perish from the face of this earth. In that case, life would no longer be worth living. I, however, want to live and I want to live long enough to see the final and complete vindication of the principles of Thomas Jefferson and the other founders of our mighty experiment in self-government, and to witness the collapse of that insolent structure of autocracy which now rears its arrogant turrets across the distant horizon of the Atlantic Ocean, and which is intent upon destroying us because it fears us and hates us and detests us as the last remaining bulwark of those ideals about the rights and duties of the average citizen which have made us what we are.

On October 12th of the year of our disgrace, 1938, a mob in New York hissed the name of their own Mayor and cheered the name of a foreign dictator. Therefore on October 14th of the same year I started writing this little book.

HENDRIK WILLEM VAN LOON
Old Greenwich, Connecticut

OUR BATTLE

I AM going to pay Adolf Hitler the only compliment I ever hope to pay him. I will confess that of our enemies, he is undoubtedly the most dangerous because he is one of those very rare persons who actually believe everything they say.

Nazi propaganda has already so completely spread throughout our own society that immediately the question will be raised: "Why single out Hitler? Why not attack Stalin and Mussolini, and how about Japan and Turkey?"

Because, while Stalin and Mussolini are surely no better than their German competitor, they are not quite as much of a direct menace to our own safety as that son of the late Alois Schicklgruber, Provisional Imperial and Royal Apostolic Customs Assistant of the Eleventh Class, who as Führer of the Third German Reich is able to dictate his will to the whole of the European continent and who would occupy a similar position in regard to the rest of the world if it were not for the existence of the United States of America.

Before I start upon this unpleasant subject, let me give myself a few words of warning. I must never allow myself to fall into the usual temptation and treat the German dictator as some sort of a painful joke. In one respect at least we had better follow his example, and take him quite as seriously as he takes himself.

7

In the second place, I would defeat my own ends if I were suspected of having a few private grievances against him. I do. He has murdered some of my best friends—cold, deliberate murder, at that. But my profession is that of an historian and historians, unfortunately, are not in a position to have any personal feelings. In that respect they are very much like doctors who have been called upon to handle a dangerous epidemic. Those poor physicians may be obliged to see some of their own dearest relatives die miserably from this ailment, but no matter what happens, they must not take sides. They must remain entirely impersonal in their attitude toward the microbe, the louse, or the mosquito which happens to be responsible for the slaughter of so many thousands of innocent people. It is their business to try and locate these malefactors and thereupon to study them until they can suggest ways and means by which these creatures can be destroyed.

But in order to do this successfully, these doctors must approach their problem in a manner of complete detachment, for they realize all along that this terrible calamity which they are called upon to fight could never have taken place if society itself had not in some serious way offended against certain elementary rules of sane living, and by its long-continued indifference and neglect had prepared a fertile soil for the rapid and triumphant growth of those enemies which now threaten its existence.

To the members of the medical profession, all microbes are alike. They are just another manifestation of that "will to live" which is the very basis of our universe. In the same way, the historian should accept those unpleasant bacilli, which occasionally attack our social systems and thereupon cause more death and destruction than a dozen outbreaks of plague or yellow fever, in a spirit of complete detachment. He should put the creatures under the microscope of common sense and should study them by the light of his past experiences. Then having duly classified them and described them in such a way that every layman can recognize them, he should do his best to tell the community how it can protect itself against any future outbreaks of this most dangerous pestilence.

I shall therefore pay as much attention to the circumstances which were responsible for this latest outbreak of "virulent autocracy" as to the germs themselves which are responsible for our present miseries.

Offhand, and in that casual way which many doctors practice when a new patient enters their office, I feel inclined to say that I shall probably come to the same conclusion as I have done so often in my studies of the past when I had to deal with the subject of autocracy. Invariably I was forced to the conclusion that AUTOCRACY WAS ALWAYS THE RESULT OF BAD DEMOCRACY.

I wish that you would read these few words again for they are at the base of all our present-day troubles. AUTOCRACY IS INVARIABLY THE RESULT OF BAD DEMOCRACY, just as typhus and cholera and smallpox are invariably the result of bad physical and economic conditions.

The Hitlers and Stalins and Mussolinis may not be to our taste and we may even loathe and hate them.

But please let us remember that we ourselves are responsible for their existence. Therefore, it is up to us to get rid of them again.

I had reached this point in writing when my son dropped in from Vermont, and after he had parked his truck (he seems to have a preference for trucks as a means of conveyance), he asked what I was doing, and I said, "I am trying to warn our people about Hitler, and here it is," and I gave him my manuscript.

He read it with care, unusual in a son reading his father's literary products, and then he handed it back to me.

"That is fine, Pa," he remarked, "and of course it is your job to use big words. But I think I know of a way in which you could have reduced this to a single paragraph and could have made at least all American housewives understand what you mean. Just tell them that if they are not careful about cleaning the place underneath the kitchen sink, very soon those big brown beetles will begin to walk around and they will have the dickens of a time getting rid of them again."

I gratefully submit this observation as proof of my long-established conviction that the world does move, at least in regard to parents and children.

As all of us know who ever had to unburden our souls to our doctor, the eminent physician, after feeling our pulse and going through a number of routine investigations, will thereupon turn father confessor and try to discover what really makes the wheels go round in the innermost sanctum of our mortal souls. His microscope and his X rays will tell him all he has got to know about our physical condition but he realizes that "matter and mind" are really one and the same thing and that a psychological maladjustment may be just as fatal as the bite of a mosquito or the wrong diet.

The human race, as a whole, is not in any way different from the individuals who go to make up the sum-total of what we rather vaguely call "humanity." The human race, too, is composed of matter and of mind and is neither all "belly" nor all "mind."

Our friends who have accepted the theory of history of the late Karl Marx as if it were part of a new kind of gospel, do not agree with this and they are eagerly trying to convince their neighbors that man is influenced in everything he does by only one motive, his need of nourishment. Within that new philosophy of life there is no room for anything but the stomach. Feed the brute and he will be happy and wealthy and wise! Fail to feed him and he will be mean, vile, and cantankerous!

In one respect they are of course entirely right. Hunger is a dreadful thing. Any sort of uncertainty about tomorrow's meals for their wives and children, if continued for too long a period of time, will drive otherwise sane people to extremes of viciousness that would make wolves and hyenas hang their heads in shame. With all that I can agree most heartily. But I cannot follow them the whole of the way, for history has continually shown me that man does not live by bread alone, but that to an equal degree he lives by his ideas, by his fairy stories, by his religious concepts, by his ideals, by all those intangible influences to

which (for the sake of greater brevity) I would like
to refer as his "illusions."

That these illusions are profoundly influenced by
the condition of his body is a statement of fact which
no reasonable citizen will undertake to dispute. When
one has been digging ditches all day long, one is not
very apt to spend the evening writing sonnets, and
sixty million Germans, who have been kept in a state
of starvation for an entire year after the cessation of
hostilities, are not going to react as normally to a sermon upon the beauty of forgiving your enemies as a
group of dear ladies who helped win the war by rais-
ing radishes for our dear boys at the front. Therefore,
I beg the followers of Herr Marx not to heave their
rhetorical brickbats at me too violently when I seem
to disagree with some of the findings of that brilliant
critic of our economic system.

Being essentially a disciple of Erasmus and Mon-
taigne and therefore a devotee of the Middle Way, I
prefer to mix the materialistic conception of history
with a bit of that common sense which still centers
around the stove in a Vermont country store or in the
taproom of an English pub, two mighty important
academies of learning rarely patronized by our students of sociology and economic theory. Yet attend-
ance at such classes, conducted by and of and for the
Average Man, would soon convince them that even in
this day and age, when the Stock Exchange has taken
the place of the altar, and when the spirit of Christmas can be expressed in just so many dollars and cents
—that even today in the year 1938 most people are
still more directly influenced by their fairy stories—

by their illusions—than by their need of food. And looking backwards across fifty centuries of written history, I make bold to state that for every hundred persons who died as a result of having asked the question, "When do we eat?" at least double that number met a much more painful end because they had ventured to ask, "What are we allowed to believe?"

Of course, I may be mistaken, for I rarely feel that I am in a position to say, "I know." The only people today who "know" are the disciples of the three new creeds, the Bolsheviks, the Fascists and the Nazis, although their "scientific conclusions" quite often impress the rest of the world more as manifestations of "wishful thinking" than as the result of serious scientific observations.

That is one of the greatest drawbacks of still being an old-fashioned Democratic Liberal. As a group we are often obliged to confess our ignorance. We may feel that we have a right to "suspect" and to "surmise" and to "assume," but we have to dispose of vast quantities of definite data before we reach the point at which we actually dare proclaim that we "know." The enemies of democracy never cease to deride us for our doubts and our misgivings. For they are soul mates to that devout champion of the early Christian Church (Tertullian, in case you want to know his name) who, when he found himself involved in a maze of irreconcilable contradictions, solved all his doubts and difficulties by quietly stating: "All this is incredible and that is just the reason why I shall believe it."

When an individual or a nation has reached that point of willful surrender of its own independent power of reasoning, then there is nothing more to be said, for after a man has told you that white is black and that black is white and that nothing you may say will ever be able to shake him in his opinion that black is white and white is black, then all further argument comes abruptly to an end. There is nothing to do but to say "yes" and change the subject.

Therefore, that which is democracy's strongest factor (in the eyes of all those who can see salvation only in the maintenance of our democratic illusion)— a generous willingness to discuss and inquire and examine and probe until a reasonable answer shall have been found which will satisfy the reasonable majority of all citizens—that very same strength becomes a definite weakness in the eyes of our opponents and by every possible means at their disposal (either fair or foul but most foul) they will thereupon try to get hold of the least intelligent part of our community at large and to convince these unfortunate citizens that democracy is nothing but a futile debating society which wastes its time in useless discussions, while autocracy "gets things done." And not infrequently they will hint that one of the first things "to get done" is to go after these doubters and debaters and hang them from the nearest lamppost.

I mention this because it has a direct bearing upon the events of the day. We are adherents of the Illusion of Free Speech. We believe in it as one of the essentials of a democratic form of government. Yet our enemies to whom we continue to grant this privilege abuse it by a form of propaganda which has only one purpose—to destroy a form of government which grants even its most dangerous enemies the right to give free expression to their views. What are we to do under such circumstances? I do not know. It is all very puzzling and perplexing.

The Nazis and the Fascists, not to forget the ubiquitous and noisy disciples of Moscow, are rapidly driving us to the conclusion that some day, in sheer self-preservation, we may have to follow their example or run the risk of seeing everything in which we believe be completely destroyed by those who use their "freedom of expression" to deny it to all others. It is the most perplexing and puzzling situation in which we have ever found ourselves. Perhaps you can provide me with the correct answer. I confess that I don't know.

But let me go back to what we were discussing a moment ago. I think that we were trying to find a solution to that age-old problem of "What do men live by?" and I had told you that according to my own views, "Men live only partly by bread and butter, but mostly by their illusions." Having discussed this question in great detail in several other books, I shall not here enumerate those historical facts which I could use to build up my case and to show you that historically speaking, all the evidence is entirely on my side.

I realize that I am writing this at a moment when a terrific crisis has overtaken the world, a crisis more serious than any other that has occurred since the end of the fifth century of our era, when the Roman government was no longer able to maintain itself in the ancient capital of the Empire and transferred the center of government from Rome to the city of Ravenna, which being situated in the marshy plains of eastern Italy was less open to a surprise attack from the Barbarians.

If you and I live another ten years, I feel convinced that we shall see a similar move on the part of the British government. For the London of the twentieth century is quite as vulnerable as the Rome of the fifth, only this time the danger will come from the air and not from the land or even the sea. The Nazi flying machines will take the place of the marauding horsemen of the Goths and Vandals, and since London is within easy striking distance from the German frontier, whereas Berlin is far removed from the air bases of England, it will soon prove a hopeless task to defend the center of the British Empire from raids on the part of the German bombers.

Therefore there will be no other way out but to remove all the governmental agencies from the bank of the Thames to some less exposed spot along the banks of the St. Lawrence River, as the Romans fled from the banks of the Tiber, first to the shores of the Adriatic and afterwards to the Bosporus. It is therefore well within the realm of possibilities that we shall see the sleepy little town of Ottawa become the residence of the British royal family and hear that what remains of the British Empire after Adolf Hitler gets through with it will henceforth be ruled from the heart of the New World.

Incidentally, this will put us face to face with a very complicated situation. For if we still believe in the Monroe Doctrine (and on the whole, we seem to be taking a renewed interest in that most useful document), then we can hardly welcome such close proximity to a city which will be the natural target for all German attacks. There is of course the Atlantic, the dear old Atlantic, which we hear praised every day by patriots who are ignorant of their geography and who forget that airplane carriers, once they have found their way into the James Bay (the lower part of the undefended Hudson Bay), can unload a cargo of flying machines which in turn can reach Ottawa in less than two hours and Detroit and our other industrial centers in less than three hours.

The removal therefore of the British capital from England to Canada would tend to bring the European imbroglio much closer than can possibly be agreeable to us from the point of view of our own safety. But even without that nightmare, there is every reason for us to wake up to the seriousness of the situation, for Adolf Hitler has a few illusions of his own. Like all truly hysterical patients, he lives primarily by his dreams. And as he has succeeded in making his own illusions an integral part of the illusions of a constantly increasing number of his adopted fellow countrymen, these Teutonic fairy stories (this time, alas, not by the Brothers Grimm, but even grimmer!) will soon make themselves felt in even the most remote regions of the New World.

For let us remember that even after a century of waste and dissipation of our natural resources, we are still rich beyond the most exaggerated dreams of the workers in Messrs. Hitler's and Mussolini's armament factories.

Furthermore, those "have not" nations which are desperately in need of more land and a greater supply of natural resources, are constantly being encouraged by our own political strife to regard us as an easy prey. Such incidents as that which took place on Columbus Day when the Mayor of New York was hissed while the name of a foreign dictator was loudly applauded are most welcome grist for their journalistic mills, which day and night grind out anti-American propaganda for the benefit of their German and Italian readers and for their supporters on this side of the Atlantic. They despise us as they have come to despise the English, who at the most critical moment in the history of the modern world fled in panic before Adolf Hitler's threats, and the events of the last four years have clearly proven that both the Nazis and the Fascists will attack anyone whom they suspect of "moral weakness," for such weakness, especially in the eyes of the Nazis, deserves to be answered only by violence and force of arms.

As a result, regardless of what now befalls England, we are next on their program of extension, together with the rich republics of South America.

The recent fate of England and France should serve as a dreadful warning of what will happen to all those who fail to appreciate the true character of Adolf Hitler. It therefore seems highly desirable that we should stop long enough in our daily pursuits of making a more or less comfortable living and comparing the relative merits of the different Hollywood ladies and Broadway lovers, to pay some very serious attention to something which after all is a matter of paramount importance to our own future. Do we want to see the Stars and Stripes continue to fly from our revenue cutters, or do we want to have them replaced by the blood-red flag bearing the Swastika?

Personally (and God knows, I am no hero!), I would rather die in the last ditch than be a witness to such an act of insufferable degradation. All this may seem quite farfetched. Granted. But if anyone should have told you three months ago that a British Prime Minister would gratefully and willingly take orders from an Austrian ex-corporal, what would you have done? You would have told your informant to stop being funny!

I am not being funny. Read your daily newspapers. Read them carefully and above all, try to read a little between the lines. Then you will realize the desperate seriousness of the situation in which we, the people of America, find ourselves as a result of that agreement of Munich, which was a deliberate and most cowardly betrayal of the cause of Democracy and which future historians will denounce as "the second Treaty of Versailles."

Here, quite naturally, you will ask me why, in all this discussion, do I make so little mention of Russia and why do I stress Hitler and Mussolini (especially the former) as those against whom we shall have to guard if we wish to maintain our independence? I assure you that I am not being inspired by any love for the present occupant of the ancient palace of the Kremlin. I have my reasons to regard Russia as a minor evil.

In the first place, for a reason as old as dictatorship itself, the instinctive fear of all tyrants for their associates and friends, Stalin has so completely destroyed the power of his own nation that for a long time to come we need not worry about any military action on the part of the Soviets. And in the second place, Russia is the largest country in the world and it is greatly underpopulated. The Russians can expand for several hundred years to come, and even after that they will still have plenty of room for many coming generations. Russia, therefore, will not be clamoring for more room in the sun (like Germany and Italy), for it has plenty of room, both in the sun and also, as Mr. Stalin's opponents know only too well, in the snow.

We have quite a number of Communists in this country, for our government-subsidized organizations are full of them. But they are still a purely domestic trouble, and if Representative Dies and his fellow inquisitors will only refrain from using them as convenient red herrings with which to divert our attention from the menace of Fascism and Nazism, I think that we shall be completely able to handle that problem without calling out the reserves. The local police and our own sensible citizens (of which, God be praised! we still have a large number in spite of our reactionaries, who are the Bolsheviks' best friends)—they will be fully able to cope with the greatly overadvertised Bolshevik menace.

There remain our parlor Bolsheviks, pleasantly financed by papa's millions and sustained by mamma's social position. But with a return of normal economic conditions, they too will evaporate or take jobs and do some really useful work and cease to be a nuisance and an irritation.

There is of course always a chance that Russia will make common cause with the Third Reich. But before that happens (and stranger things than that have happened!), the Russian military machine will have to be greatly improved, especially within the field of its air force. By the way, I got this information not from Colonel Lindbergh or Lady Astor, but directly from the Finns. It is their business to know, as their own safety depends entirely upon a thorough knowledge about conditions in Russia. And therefore, for several years to come, Russia, as far as we ourselves are concerned, is out of the picture, and just now I am interested only in our own fate.

This may sound selfish but a little enlightened self-interest in the year 1938 won't do any of us any harm. So suppose we let it go at that and proceed to discuss our relations with Germany and Italy.

Here is another point which I must stress if we want to see the developments of the last fifteen years in their right proportion. Both Fascism and Nazism, although of course they are the result of general conditions which greatly favored their development, are essentially the work of two outstanding personalities. They are both of them the reflected shadows of two ambitious and highly dynamic human beings. Allah be praised, these two men hate each other with a bitter hatred and despise each other with an ill-concealed contempt. As long as certain political necessities shall force them to make common cause, Hitler and Mussolini will play ball together. They would be very foolish if they were to do otherwise. But the moment the diplomats of the democratic nations (our own by preference, for the English ones are always off on some week-end holiday)—the moment the diplomacy of the Western nations succeeded in making Mussolini understand that it would serve his own interests much better if he were to let the axis stop at his side of the Alps, the Duce would do so with almost indecent haste, and it probably would be one of the happiest days of his life.

And in the second place, there is the difference in the temperaments of the two nations. The Fascist Italian is (to us) much less dangerous than the Nazi German because, even in the blackest of black shirts and with the highest of high boots and brandishing the most dangerous of all dangerous daggers, he still realizes that he is engaged in some amusing revival of his ancestral *commedia dell' arte*. He is really "playacting."

Fascism has never really developed a regular literature of its own which tries seriously to interpret the deeper philosophic meaning of that strange creed. Recently, under pressure from Berlin, the Italians have tried to compose a few volumes of that sort and to provide the edifice of Fascism with a sound philosophical and historical substructure. These "apologies" were so evidently written while their authors held their tongues in their cheeks, that no one has been able to take them very seriously, least of all the Italians themselves, with their instinctive sense for the absurd and the grotesque. Even that curious and unexpected outbreak of Italian anti-Semitism of a few months ago could not in any way be compared with the scrofulous labors of such men as Herr Streicher and his filthy *Stürmer*. One felt all the time that Il Duce, desperately pressed for money, was making a grab for the riches accumulated by his Hebrew subjects and that he would be quite contented to drop the matter the moment they gave him a few millions as "a patriotic donation."

In Italy (let us keep this fact clearly in mind), the revolutionary movement did not arise from a preconceived and definite philosophy of life as it did in Germany. The Fascist movement was something that happened almost overnight and quite instinctively, and as something that almost seems to have been made to order to prove that I was right when I said that "Autocracy is invariably the result of bad democracy."

Let us make a little detour and pay some attention to the state of affairs in Italy immediately after the Great War.

Italy had had no desire to enter into the war. Indeed, it had so little interest in the struggle that it used a very flimsy excuse for the nonfulfillment of its obligations toward the other two members of the Triple Alliance and for declaring itself neutral. This neutrality lasted as long as London and Paris needed to concoct a clever scheme by which the Roman government could be persuaded to see that "Right in this case was on the side of the allied powers."

To this day, no one knows exactly what London and Paris, in their hour of need, offered to the statesmen who were in power in Italy in the fall of the year 1914, but it must have been much more than this poor country obtained when the spoils of Versailles were distributed among the victors. Together with the Japanese and the Arabs, the Italians were left holding the bag, and the bag was empty. Arthur James Balfour may have been a great philosopher, but the author of the famous *Foundations of Belief* seems to have been ignorant of the Ninth Commandment which has something very pertinent to say upon the subject of "bearing false witness."

As for the man at the head of the British government during the end of the war, he was really a sublimated sort of ward politician and the question, "When is a promise not a promise?" was answered by him in the fashion common to all the members of his tribe. A promise, according to his way of thinking, was not a promise when it happened to interfere with your own interests.

Remain the other gentlemen responsible for the Versailles disaster—Clemenceau, Poincaré, Orlando and our own Woodrow Wilson. Clemenceau was an old man, kept alive solely by onion soup and hate. Poincaré was the French bureaucrat, raised to the nth degree. His views were restricted by the Pyrenees on the south, the Jura and Vosges mountains on the east, and the Bay of Biscay on the west. Rarely has a man with such a completely one-track mind held such a powerful position. I know of course that he was not one of the actual signers of the treaty, but it was the Poincaré influence even more than that of the real signers of that notorious document which was responsible for the disastrous consequences of that piece of illuminated parchment, signed among such general jubilations in that same Hall of Mirrors in the palace of Louis XIV in which, a generation before, Bismarck had proclaimed the King of Prussia as Emperor of that German Empire which came to an end with the defeat of the Kaiser's armies.

As for poor Woodrow Wilson, his cause was lost the moment he set foot on the ship that was to carry him to Europe. He was in every way unfit for the task he undertook with such high hopes and in a spirit of such complete confidence in the ultimate triumph of right over might.

A college professor and a college president, he had never known his fellow men as they really are. He was a confirmed devotee of that amiable but dangerous American creed which takes it for granted that all people are instinctively endowed with enough "good will" to make them safe and pleasant neighbors. "Get them together and talk to them and appeal to the best there is in them, and you will find all people willing to come to a decent and sensible agreement."

Shades of Berchtesgaden and Munich! Will democracies never learn that there are people who are as insensitive to any sort of appeal to either reason or common decency as the most destructive forces of nature, men who have no more human feeling in their hearts than an earthquake or a hurricane or a forest fire and who could no more be moved from the narrow path they have chosen for themselves than a flow of lava or a tidal wave? Talk to them all you want, reason with them for half a year, appeal to their sense of mercy, and you will get no more reaction than I would have got six weeks ago if I had gone out on the porch of my house in Old Greenwich to stop the wall of water that engulfed the whole of the Connecticut coast by making it listen to Dickens' *Christmas Carol* or some other lovely piece of sentimental prose.

Woodrow Wilson would have shivered were the poor man still here to read this statement. Our war president was a sort of Candide on a Presbyterian basis. Everything to him (until the last years of his life) was for the best in the best of all possible worlds, as it still is with millions of his fellow Americans who have spent all their lives in a dream world of Mother, Home and Heaven. They can observe sparks of sweetness and light in a cage filled with jackals or hyenas.

As a result, the jackals and hyenas quickly devoured their great and good friend from across the waters and left him to die amidst the bleached bones of his own noble ideals, a disappointed and brokenhearted man, who argued and reasoned to the last moment instead of reminding his European colleagues that America had won the war for them and that America was now going to dictate its own sort of peace, or otherwise it would take its armies and its navy and its well-filled treasure chest home, and then where would they be? They would have had to accept his terms and they knew it.

And so the Japanese and the Arabs and the Italians who had done yeoman service for the Allies and more especially for the English—these poor dupes of Downing Street were sent home with further high-sounding if hazy promises, but not with any of those concrete gains which alone could have satisfied the mass of the people for the sacrifices they had just made.

In the case of Italy, the rewards were especially disappointing. The old men of Versailles were interested in revenge and in plunder, but not in geography. They had come to Paris accompanied by a small army of historical, ethnological and geographical experts, but they never seem to have consulted a single one of these, for their final rearrangement of the map of the world makes the territorial outlines established by the Congress of Vienna of the year 1815 look like something divinely inspired.

Italy had suffered terribly during the Great War. To the majority of the Italian people it had been an unpopular war, for why should any Italian peasant or macaroni manufacturer lift a finger (let alone a hand holding a musket!) for that same France which only two generations before had deprived his country of Nice and the greater part of the Maritime Alps and which had cheated the immortal Garibaldi out of his just rewards by sending an army to prevent the young Italian kingdom from occupying its logical capital, the ancient city of Rome?

As for the British Empire, that too meant very little in the life of the average Italian, who felt his country completely bottled up by the fortifications of Gibraltar and the warships of Alexandria and who for more than two centuries past had had no other prospect of advancement in this world than working as either a butler or a cook for some haughty milord who lived comfortably in some ancient Umbrian villa or Piedmontese castle and who sometimes was willing to pay him as much as ten dollars a month for his services.

And now, badly equipped and miserably commanded by incompetent officers, these poor devils had been driven into a war against their own former allies and when it was all over and there was nothing to do but to tend the endless cemeteries around Gorizia and along the banks of the Isonzo River, these patient little fellows, who are totally unsuited for modern warfare, were told that as a reward for their futile sacrifices they would receive the province of Trieste and a slice of southern Tyrol (with an indigestible population of some 100,000 loyal German-Austrians). They did not obtain the city of Fiume to which they felt they had a right as the population was predominantly Italian. And as for colonies—a matter of life and death to a race as prolific as the Italians—not one scrap! The former German possessions in Africa and the Pacific area were parceled out among the French and the English and such English dominions as Australia and New Zealand and the Union of South Africa.

The result, therefore, of the Great War, as far as Italy was concerned, was national bankruptcy, millions of unemployed and millions of ex-soldiers who were left in a state of misery which one must have seen in order to appreciate it.

Here I must refer you once more to a statement which I made on a previous page in which I compared the outbreaks of Bolshevism, Fascism and Nazism with epidemics of cholera or yellow fever or some other dangerous disease, which will occur when a prolonged neglect on the part of the health officers (the politicians and those responsible for the economic status of any given country) have so weakened the national organism that it has lost all power of resistance.

Italy was therefore an ideal spot for a violent outbreak of some terrible social malady. In the beginning it looked as if the microbe from Moscow would be victorious and as if Italy would turn toward Bolshevism. And then, just when the rich people and the middle classes, in their hopeless despair, were ready to surrender to the inevitable and to accept some sort of a compromise with the emissaries of Lenin, behold! there appeared one Benito Mussolini, until then chiefly known as a militant radical, who now almost overnight changed the entire aspect of the case by providing the Italian people with a counterirritant, so strong and effective that the Moscovite bacillus was completely eradicated in less than a year.

The savior of Italy thereupon made himself the head of his party and that party came to be known as the Fascist party, from the *fasces* or bundle of rods which had been the sign of authority of the lifeguards of the magistrates of the old Roman republic and empire and which was adapted as the symbol of the new masters of the Italian kingdom. And by the way, if you want to know what these *fasces* look like, take a handful of money out of your pocket, if you are still an economic royalist. For some queer reason, we have put these bundles of rods on the reverse of our own dimes.

I fully disagree with the doctrine now so commonly held by those who believe in the materialistic interpretation of history—that history makes great men but that great men do not make history. My good friends of the opposite camp reason that all great leaders were merely the result of circumstances. According to them, a Napoleon or a Peter the Great or a Joan of Arc or an Abraham Lincoln were really quite insignificant in themselves, but were made what they eventually became, because the conditions under which they lived forced them to play the roles that since then have become associated with their names. In other words, for lack of a Napoleon or an Abraham Lincoln, familiar to us all, someone by the name of Jean Chose or John Jones would suddenly have stepped forward and would have done all the things accomplished by the authentic Napoleon or Lincoln. Such problems, like everything else connected with our hopelessly irrational and illogical human race, are very complicated. It is quite true that if there had been no French Revolution, Napoleon might have spent his days as an obscure captain of artillery in some provincial nest of France and Lincoln, save for our Civil War, might never have been known outside of the state in which he practiced his haphazard profession as a country lawyer and amateur politician.

Granted. But if there had been no Napoleon or

Abraham Lincoln to take hold of affairs at the precise moment when they did and in the manner in which they did, the French Revolution under Jean Chose or John Jones might very well have ended in complete anarchy with a victory for the reactionary powers of Europe, while the philatelists of today would be obliged to collect Confederate stamps as well as those of the Republic of the United States.

We need not go as far back as Thomas Carlyle, who saw the whole of the past as a pageant of glorious heroes, to realize that the "exceptional man" (whether good, bad or indifferent, but "exceptional") has always been one of the most decisive factors in the history of mankind. And no matter whether we like Benito Mussolini or hate and despise him, he is there! He is what his Latin ancestors called a *brutum factum* —a brutal fact which no amount of wishful thinking can reason away.

As for the Italian Führer, he shares his unusual name with quite a different character—with the gentle Benito d'Espinoza. But whereas the pious parents of that Portuguese fugitive from the Fascist violence of seventeenth-century Spain were undoubtedly thinking of the original meaning of Baruch, the "Blessed One," the father of Il Duce, a blacksmith and a radical—(anybody of an independent turn of mind in the year 1883 was a "radical," as he still is in many parts of our country in the year 1938)—that elder Mussolini was a stanch Italian patriot and therefore a bitter enemy of the House of Habsburg. He was also politically minded and remembered that some sixteen years before a certain Benito had killed a Habsburg prince.

That was Benito Juarez, the full-blooded Indian who as president of Mexico had executed Maximilian of Habsburg, the ill-fated usurper of the Mexican throne and a brother of the late Francis Joseph.

It was an interesting choice, for the godchild, Benito Mussolini, has most fully lived up to his Christian name. He is of the same tough fiber as his Zapotec godfather. He is bursting forth with virile energy. He is not only a man's man but also, apparently, quite a woman's man. And on occasions he can be quite as cruel and as ruthless as his Mexican namesake. But these qualities are combined with an unscrupulous shrewdness that is entirely Italian and smacks of the writings of the late Niccolò Machiavelli. And here the comparison ends for Benito Mussolini—unlike Benito Juarez—was not educated for the priesthood and his early training was not given him by the Church. His father, the village atheist, would never have tolerated this, for he hated all priests and was forever at odds with the clergy of his town. Mussolini's mother, on the other hand, was a gentle schoolteacher and a deeply religious woman. She, too, left her mark upon her brilliant but untractable son and, as a result, there is a quality in Mussolini's character which never quite allows us to predict what he will do next, whether he will occupy Vatican City and send the Pope to the Lipari Islands (the sun-scorched Siberia of the Fascist state) or whether he will humbly kneel before the Holy Father and proclaim himself a loyal son of the Church.

It will be well to keep this in mind during the coming months. Mussolini has always been an uncertain factor in any political setup. If Hitler, who lets himself be guided by his impulses, should at any moment seriously interfere with the plans of his Italian confederate, Mussolini would turn against his beloved Adolf as savagely as he has turned against all his other friends who at one moment or another failed to see eye to eye with their leader. He is a much better educated man than Hitler and his range of knowledge, especially within the fields of history and literature, is infinitely wider. He therefore knows enough of the past to avoid at least a few of the errors of the present, which eventually will destroy Adolf Hitler, as they have destroyed all other previous dictators who thought of themselves as "special cases" and therefore exempt from the influence of those cosmic forces which shape the lives of all of us.

At the age of eighteen, young Benito passed his examinations as an elementary-school teacher. But trying to instruct the dull-witted, undernourished children of a little provincial Italian town, soon drove him to exasperation, and so he took the few lire he had saved and went to Switzerland and supported himself by manual labor. There he had another experience which Hitler never had. He came in close and intimate contact with the "real article," with the mechanic and the carpenter and the blacksmith, who pay for what they get, who bring up decent families and who are neither saints nor devils, but plain, ordinary, everyday sons of toil.

I most heartily recommend a few years of this sort of existence to all our future statesmen. For then—and only then—will they learn something really worth-while about a class of people which will play the most important role in the political and social and economic development of the next two or three centuries. They will then come to appreciate the quiet courage of these fellows, who hammer away at their workbench in a garage and perform intricate if dull jobs in manufacturing plants and on the whole are contented enough with their fate. They will be astonished at the tremendous thirst for knowledge that exists among these men, some of whom will go for weeks without a bottle of beer or a much-needed package of cigarettes to buy some book of which they have heard and which they want to read for themselves. They will then discover an amount of native if undeveloped intelligence that makes a great many of our professors and professional men look like hopeless and pale amateurs. But, at the same time, they will soon recognize that the majority of the members of the laboring classes are in no essential way different from those who employ them and that one can be just as generous or just as mean, just as kindhearted or just as nasty, just as brilliant or just as commonplace, in a pair of overalls as in a white collar.

That dangerous lack of firsthand information which dooms the efforts of so many of our reformers, who know their laboring classes only from Congressional reports and the weeklies of Social Uplift and which is responsible for a great deal of muddleheaded legislation, is at least one mistake which Mussolini never made. It may well account for the fact that although he has often treated the Italian laborers with great harshness, he has never quite lost touch with them and that they have never risen in open rebellion against him. For verily, the Italian workingman does not sleep on a bed of roses. He enjoys about as much freedom as a galley slave at the pulling end of an oar. He is not allowed to join a union. He is not permitted to go on strike. He has to take what is given him by the State and humbly say, "Thank you." At the bidding of his master, he must drop his tools and pick up a gun and risk life and limb in the God-forsaken jungles of Ethiopia or among the barren mountains of Spain, fighting in quarrels which affect his own interests only very distantly. But somehow or other, Mussolini still has their confidence. They may grumble and grouch (and they do), but all the time, having been one of them, he seems able to speak their own language and they continue to like him, in spite of what he has done to them, and still may do in the future.

The Swiss, with their proverbial lack of imagination, completely failed to appreciate this eager-eyed immigrant who spent his days working at an anvil and his nights in the public library, cramming up on socialism and history, and who in spite of his busy days found time to organize his fellow workingmen and to incite them into drastic demands for better living conditions and a more human form of existence. When it became clear that this foreigner was the driving force behind a large number of strikes, they arrested him, threw him out of one canton after the other, and finally expelled him altogether from the territory of the Swiss Confederacy.

His own country was just as unenthusiastic about his efforts. When he popped up in the Romagna (that ancient and miserably neglected part of central Italy which still suffered from the aftereffects of having been for many centuries a part of the States of the Church) and began to organize the peasants and show them how to fight their grasping absentee landlords, the Italian government promptly arrested this exschoolteacher and condemned him to a term in prison.

As soon as he got out, and while still under police surveillance as a "dangerous revolutionary," he moved to Trent and became the editor of a Socialist newspaper. At the same time, he learned German, became a voracious reader of everything Nietzsche had ever written, and came in contact with several leaders of the Irredentist party, that patriotic movement which hoped to restore unto Italy all those territories which had been lost during the centuries when Italy had been under foreign domination.

Maybe it was the uncompromising Nietzsche, with his belief in salvation through the unselfish services of those truly born to be leaders, or maybe it was the rising antagonism he began to feel toward his fellow Socialists who were more and more drifting into the camp of the bourgeoisie, but gradually young Mussolini grew farther and farther apart from the orthodox teachings of Karl Marx and drifted into the camp of Georges Sorel. This remarkable man, whose name is anathema to most of our own legislators, was a French engineer who, exasperated at the corruption and greed

and cowardice and slipshod methods of the French
parliamentary system of the year 1868, had preached
a gospel of open revolt against all democratic forms
of government. To him they appeared as the final
triumph of organized mediocrity, and being a clever
writer he had become the best-known advocate of
that form of systematic violence which Pierre-Joseph
Proudhon, the enemy of French parliamentary government, had first expounded under the name of
Syndicalism.

Both Proudhon and Sorel had been inspired by a
truly religious fervor in their efforts to drag the long-
suffering laboring classes from that slough of despond
in which they had wallowed ever since the beginning
of the industrial revolution almost a hundred years
before. In their works, Benito Mussolini, in search of
a new illusion to replace the faith of his childhood
days (which he had long since lost), at last found what
he wanted. He broke definitely with the Socialist
party, which had lost its former fervor for the under-
dog, and following Sorel's example, he too declared
war upon the established order of things as represented by the parliamentary system of his native
country.

In view of his subsequent career as a superpatriot,
forever waving the flag and rattling a sword, his first
debut as an independent Socialist was a very curious
one. He violently opposed the expedition which just
then was being planned against Tripoli. He declared
himself unalterably opposed to every form of foreign
aggression while the country itself was still in that
state of picturesque but abject poverty which was a

heritage from the days of the Middle Ages and the result of four centuries of rule by Austrian and Spanish princelings.

"Improvement begins at home," became his slogan, and he screamed it with such indiscriminate fury from every soapbox that soon he was once more arrested and sent to jail. This time he got five months. The enforced isolation did not in any way break his spirits. The moment he was released, he undertook to edit the Socialist paper *Avanti* and he put so much life into that sheet that the circulation within a very few months jumped from a mere forty thousand to over a hundred thousand, quite a respectable number for any European paper of the more conservative sort, let alone a Socialist one.

At this point in his career, Mussolini still seems to have believed in the "masses." If only the masses could be made to understand the necessity for "combined action," he felt sure that Italy would soon regain her old status as a proud and prosperous nation. But no matter how eloquently he tried to hammer this idea into their heads, the masses remained indifferent. The masses, as usual, were composed of ordinary "average men" and the ordinary average man is rarely interested in those ideas which have only a distant bearing upon his own immediate interests. Not all of them, as I told you only a moment ago. The "unusual ones," the "exceptional ones" will perform tasks of herculean endurance to gain an education and help in the work of pushing this world forward along the road of progress. But the others will never move unless someone actually pushes them and pushes them hard.

And here was this young editor, drunk with the glories of his ancestral country, those glories of which he saw the ruined evidence on every highway and crossroad, but which meant nothing or less than nothing to his neighbors, except perhaps as a source of easy revenue by means of selling picture postal cards or hiring out rooms to tourists.

A man who had trained himself to think in the terms of Nietzsche's appeal to the sublime and who had come to think in terms of an enlightened and unselfish leadership, could under these circumstances come to only one conclusion—that he himself was the chosen one, that he himself was the Moses called upon to lead his people from the House of Bondage. But before he had had time to develop these ideas any further, the Great War broke out.

Benito had inherited his father's hatred for the House of Habsburg and he loudly fulminated against any sort of co-operation with the traditional Austrian enemy. The *Avanti* threw its influence against observing the stipulations of the Triple Alliance. As a syndicalist and a pacifist, Mussolini might have favored the idea of taking part in a war which (as most people in every part of the world then seriously believed) was to be the war to put an end to all war. But on no account must a single drop of Italian blood be spilled to further the cause of the detested Habsburg dynasty.

I also suspect that Benito Mussolini, a confirmed realist, must have realized that Italy was in no way prepared to take part in a real war. The members of the parliamentary debating society in Rome had been too busy with their own interests to devote much of either their own time or the taxpayers' money to serious military preparations. The millions duly appropriated for the army and navy had been spent, but they had not been invested in those guns and submarines and bayonets and hand grenades which have long since replaced personal valor and private initiative. They had for the greater part found their way into the pockets of the legislators.

When finally the Roman government concluded its bargain with the highest bidders (London and Paris), the inevitable came to pass. Mussolini, who had volunteered for service, although as the editor of a newspaper he was exempt, went into the trenches as a private, and in February of the year 1917 he was so badly wounded by the explosion of a trench mortar that he was forced to spend several months in a hospital. As soon as he was dismissed, he went back to his editorial labors. Even after the disaster of Caporetto, when most Italians lost heart, he unceasingly preached "resistance unto the last man!" However, at the last moment, the Allies repaired the breach in the Italian front, the war came to an end, and Italy, ruined in its man power and finances, then discovered that it had been grossly betrayed by its new friends and had gained nothing for the deliberate betrayal of its old allies.

Mussolini's wrath now assumed titanic proportions and he let it be known that he was ready to clean house, to turn the parliamentary scoundrels out and to show his people the road to salvation. Even then, however, few observers could have foretold in what direction that road to salvation would lead, for when the Bolsheviks (then in complete control of the situation) seized all Italian factories and decided that henceforth the workers would own all the means of production, Mussolini seemed to regard such a step as the logical result of that syndicalistic form of agitation of which he all along had been a most ardent advocate and for several months he was actually on the side of Communism.

But soon the hopeless lack of discipline and the absence of all true patriotism on the part of the Communist leaders began to irritate and annoy him most seriously. When the Italian Communists tried to destroy their opponents by a systematically organized series of murders, this irritation rapidly developed into an exasperation which made all further understanding with Moscow impossible. Once more the perils inherent in all forms of popular government made themselves manifest. Once again democracy betrayed itself. Parliament had lost the ball. Communism had picked it up and now fumbled it. It therefore was anybody's ball. For a while the poor thing (authority) was kicked around in the mud—one day by one party, the next day by another. Until Mussolini did what some energetic person will invariably do under such circumstances. He picked it up, tucked it under his arm and told the others: "You had your chance. You lost it. Now it is mine and it stays mine."

Together with the party he had recruited from among his fellow war veterans, small groups of exceedingly hard-boiled young men accustomed to violence and eager to redeem their former defeats and give their lives for any sort of ideal that appealed to them, Mussolini rushed from one victory to the next and in the year 1922, after the famous march on Rome, he was recognized by the vast majority of all Italians as the savior of their country and became the real ruler of the Italian peninsula.

With a much better sense of "the historically expedient" than Hitler (the result of his knowledge of the past), he carefully refrained from breaking the tradition which linked the House of Savoy with Italy's struggle for independence. He never officially touched the prerogatives of the King as the real head of the nation. He continually goes out of his way to stress the fact that he is only one of His Majesty's most obedient servants, although every child knows that Victor Emmanuel, while still ruling by the grace of God, is now merely the occupant of a throne which he holds by the grace of a blacksmith's son from the province of Emilia.

Up to now, this reads rather like a hymn of praise of the good Duce and everything he has done for his native land. If the chapter ended right here, we might even feel that America has missed a lot by not having a little Mussolini of its own. But that was only the beginning of the story and autocracy is in many respects like matrimony. At first it works beautifully. Then come the everyday cares: children which have to be fed and washed and bills which have to be paid and meals which have to be served at regular hours and an endless number of commonplace but unavoidable chores which must be taken care of when there are so many other and much more agreeable things to do.

These are the real tests which will show whether the two contracting parties were fit for each other and for their jobs and can practice enough mutual forbearance, understanding, and patience to see their venture to a successful end.

Today, after sixteen years of Fascist rule, let us examine what progress has been made, in how far the Italian people are better off than they were before and whether all the sacrifices they have been asked to make and their complete surrender of every form of personal and collective liberty are balanced by a corresponding sum in happiness and prosperity?

That Fascism was unavoidable—that something like it had to come to save the nation from anarchy and civil war—that, I believe is something upon which all reasonable Italians in the year 1922 most heartily agreed and with which we ourselves can concur. After a flood or an earthquake, even the most democratic community is forced to call out the militia to prevent the hoodlum elements of society from establishing a rule of gangsterdom in which nobody's life is any longer safe and in which private property is at the mercy of every cutthroat with a blackjack. But when the waters have receded and the roads have been repaired and the houses have been rebuilt, then we in America have always hastened to send the soldiers back to their homes and to leave the maintenance of order to the regularly established civil authorities.

And that is where we, in our democracy, differ from the autocratic nations of Europe. We may be wrong, but suppose that for a moment we look at the record of the Fascist government since it declared a perpetual state of siege. Granted all the good things Mussolini has accomplished, would we care to follow the Italian example?

Suppose we draw up a little statement after the pattern of those well-known documents your bank sends you at the end of each month—so much to the good and so much to the bad. Here is the account of Benito Mussolini, as of the twenty-seventh of October of the year 1938.

On the credit side we must put a greatly increased sense of self-respect on the part of the Italian people, a much greater pride in their past achievements, a much deeper consciousness of the role a rejuvenated Italian Empire may still play in the history of the world. Some of this of course is rather bombastic and perhaps a little childish, for Empires never repeat themselves. They were too much the result of circumstances, over which the people themselves had no control, and once these circumstances have changed, that opportunity is gone forever. But the average Italian, through the labors of Benito Mussolini, is no longer Tony the Bootblack, but feels himself a lineal descendant of Antonius Calcolarius, who as a member of the XXVIIth regiment of the line carried his shield and sword from one end of the civilized world to the other and who died a glorious death in the forests of northern Europe, holding his own against the ancestors of those same wild Teutons who today are supposed to be his dearly beloved friends and allies.

Physically too the modern Italian has greatly benefited. He now can go to school. More than that, whether he likes it or not, he has got to go to school. He no longer is a dejected, malaria-shaken peasant, shivering in a filthy mud hut in some unhealthy swamp, for the swamps are gone. At long last, the age-old marshes have been dried up, and they have been turned into grain fields and help to make the Italian kingdom self-supporting and independent from other nations, so that in case of war, Italy does not have to fear a blockade as it did in the fall of the year 1914, when the prospect of such an action on the part of the British fleet was one of the contributory causes which forced Italy to take the side of the Allies.

Then too, for the first time in its history since the days of the Empire, Italy has decent roads and cheap means of transportation. The lack of coal for manufacturing purposes has been overcome by the harnessing of the water power of the Alps and Italy has been set free from the importation of that costly black stuff which meant such a terrific drain upon an already slender treasury.

Also a state of public order prevails which guarantees the average citizen a degree of safety he had never enjoyed before. Small wonder that every Sicilian or Neapolitan gangster found it nesessary to transfer his activities from his native land to our own republic. The Fascist police was not only active but once it had caught one of its victims, the fellow was doomed. He could no longer "approach" the judge, and mere technicalities would not save him from his fate. Sentences of solitary confinement of twenty or thirty years' duration proved a mighty deterrent to all crimes of violence—from kidnaping to highway robbery—and today Italy is about as safe a country as Sweden or Denmark.

Finally, those dank caverns that went by the name of homes and in which the greater part of the Italian peasantry had been condemned to raise its numerous offspring for so many centuries past that they hardly knew any better—those human pigsties have been replaced by a greatly improved sort of houses.

There may be other items on the credit side, such as fast modern ocean liners on which every bellhop and cabin boy is obliged to go to class for so many hours each day; a much greater honesty in all public affairs; but I think that I have enumerated enough "assets" to convince even the most ardent of our numerous local Fascists that this is no wild scream of fury against his beloved Duce.

Benito Mussolini is an autocrat. Originally he may even have been an autocrat against his own will, the result of an historical accident. But the fact remains that he is an autocrat, and autocrats simply cannot avoid acquiring some of the defects of their own virtues (as the French have it), and to this rule Il Duce is no exception. Having a very earthy streak in his make-up and being a born enemy of all forms of asceticism (Puritanism, if you like that better), he has so far most successfully avoided becoming another Hitler. He is no prig and when he is not actually playing the role of the Great Man and strutting before vast imaginary multitudes, he may, for all I know, even be able to laugh at himself. Like an Italian merchant of "genuine tortoise shell" (made in the celluloid factories of Germany), who has just sold you a very expensive and very phony cigarette case, he probably derives immense satisfaction from some of his successful coups—from putting one over on Mr. Anthony Eden in his fine clothes and with his gentlemanly airs or from exposing the hollowness and emptiness of the discussions in the gatherings of the League of Nations. Even when he breaks forth into one of his periodic outbursts of oratory and indulges in some magnificent feat of rabble-rousing (an art in which he is a past master), one always has the feeling that at the end of the speech and while his hearers are yelling themselves hoarse and are ready to attack every nation in the whole world, he might quietly turn to one of the foreign reporters whom he remembered from his own newspaper days and whisper *sotto voce*, "Well, boy, I gave them the works, didn't I? Now wait for the English papers. Old Chamberlain may be so mad he will forget to take his umbrella with him when he goes out tomorrow morning!"

But all this, while very amusing, does not change the fact that Mussolini, although officially he remains the most obedient servant of His Majesty King Emmanuel, is a dictator. He is responsible to no one but himself and to his God. As the good Lord is probably an exceedingly silent partner in this strange partnership of an ex-Syndicalist agitator and the Deity, he is not liable for his actions to anyone but Benito Mussolini and no man who ever held quite so much power within his own hands has been able to keep a sober head on his shoulders. In the end the drug of mass adulation will get them and then they cease to be ordinary human beings, for they will brook neither contradiction nor opposition.

Il Duce therefore, these last ten years, has lived in some sort of spiritual vacuum. He is no longer able to hear many things of which he should not remain ignorant. He can no longer see what he should see with his own eyes. And the Dalai Lama of Tibet is no more cut off from any direct touch with the rest of his fellow men than this former socialist spellbinder and expert in soapbox oratory.

The result of this enforced aloofness from all ordinary, everyday affairs is already beginning to make itself felt and in a most disastrous manner. Italy, for several years now, has been in constant danger of being forced into some highly precarious foreign adventure which within a few weeks may undo all the good work accomplished during the previous sixteen years. Ethiopia could easily have been turned into a disaster if England and France had been really serious in their desire to stop that filibustering expedition against the last of the independent African nations. But England and France, probably remembering their own bad records as colonial highwaymen, did not mean business. They went through the entirely empty gesture of shaking an angry finger at this unexpected rival and then bade him good luck and do whatever he liked, by the simple expedient of placing an embargo upon turnips and toy balloons and other such dangerous necessities

of war, while leaving Italy free to import all the gaso-
line and nitrates it might need to destroy the Negus.

Furthermore, they knew all along that our businessmen would continue to sell everything that could be
dumped into the hold of a ship to an Italy which upon
this occasion was suddenly able to pay cash. For while
we love peace and have more peace societies than any
other nation under the sun, we also love profits and
do not inquire too closely into the ultimate purpose
of these thousands of tons of scrap iron that leave our
ports, as long as the consignee assures us that they will
only be used for baby carriages.

But let us dispose of Benito Mussolini, so that we
can get at Adolf Hitler, for time is short and every
day we neglect to prepare our defenses we run more
risk of sharing the sad fate of England.

By and large, of course, we have much less to fear
from Il Duce than from the Führer. So far all of
Italy's efforts at expansion have run in a direction
which need not worry us, for neither the Mediterranean nor Africa will ever affect our own lives in any
direct way, unless the British government, in another
outburst of generosity, decides to give Herr Hitler a
naval base in those parts of the Portuguese colonies
which (by air) are only 1800 miles removed from the
coast of Brazil.

As for the Spanish situation, it remains so hopelessly obscure that few Americans know what to make
of it except that by now it has become quite clear to
all military observers that the Italian soldiers could
run just as fast backwards at Guadalajara as they had

done during their famous marathon at Caporetto in the year 1917.

Speaking of Spain brings up the question: Should the United States ever take a direct and active part in European affairs? Opinions upon this subject differ according to the times and the circumstances, but there are many precedents which clearly show that we may again be forced to do so. A generation ago, the prolonged neglect of Cuba by the Spanish authorities and the horror we felt at the tortures which the noble Castilians chose to inflict upon their unfortunate subjects in that lovely island, finally made us send our navy down there and put an end to this nightmare. And during the last hundred years, whenever a European government, such as Czarist Russia or Turkey under Abdul Hamid, misbehaved itself in such a way that the outcries of the victims could be heard all the way across the ocean, there arose such a storm of indignation in our land that the authorities in Washington had no choice but to take drastic diplomatic steps to put an end to these atrocities.

Indeed, in the days when we had not yet grown as rich as we are today and therefore were under no obligation to cater to everybody's good will to maintain our favorable balance of exports, and when we still felt a very decided pride in being plain, ordinary Americans—yes, in those days, we sometimes dared to interfere in European affairs in a manner which would greatly have shocked the superpolite officials of our present Department of State. I refer readers who are curious to know the details about one of those incidents to the correspondence between our Secretary of State, Mr. Daniel Webster, and the Austrian Chargé d'Affaires, Herr Hülsemann, in regard to the hideous way in which the Habsburgs had avenged themselves upon their vanquished Hungarian subjects. But then, other times, other ways, as the recent attitude of England's rulers toward the leader of Nazi Germany shows only too clearly and also too painfully.

When, shortly after his atrocious campaign in Hungary in 1848, the Austrian general Haynau (known to history as "Butcher Haynau") visited London on a social visit and was almost beaten to death by the angry workingmen of Messrs. Barclay and Perkins, the well-known brewers, and when a complaint was lodged with the British Foreign Office, Vienna was curtly informed that it had no reason to expect otherwise, when it had the bad taste to let a creature like Haynau visit civilized countries. And Vienna had to accept this rebuff without a word of protest, as it was obliged to do shortly afterwards when this same military gentleman was almost lynched by an infuriated mob in Brussels.

Mr. Chamberlain, I believe, is in the hardware business and not in the brewery business, but I am sure that Messrs. Barclay and Perkins (who are still doing business at the same stand, near Mr. William Shakespeare's old theater) will be delighted to show him the premises on which a militant democracy showed its opinion of the Habsburg brand of autocracy. Such a visit, after Berchtesgaden and Munich, might not be flattering to the pride of the British Prime Minister, but it might prove a useful lesson in what we could call "applied history."

One further point deserves to be mentioned here. I refer to Signor Mussolini's way of handling labor, for our own labor unions are greatly incensed at the suppression of all freedom in the autocratic nations of Europe. History has clearly shown us that there are no worse slave drivers in the world than those ex-slaves who finally have become masters. And the most inexcusable sweatshop methods always seem to prevail on the premises of those gentlemen who until very recently had themselves belonged to the class of the sweated. From a purely academic point of view, it is therefore very interesting to study an ex-laboring man after he has become the head of the state and is called upon to deal with his former buddies.

Benito Mussolini, the former advocate of violence as a means of bringing the Marxian class struggle to a speedy and successful conclusion, has long since abjured these heresies of his younger years. Today he is the prophet of the corporate state which he established in Italy at a time when his rival across the Alps was merely a funny little beer-garden spellbinder with a trick mustache whom nobody would take seriously.

This corporate state is based upon the presumption that there is no sound reason why the employer and the employee should regard each other as enemies. On the contrary, according to the theory which today prevails in Italy and Germany, the man in the overalls and the man in the celluloid collar have the same interests and therefore they should be able to work together in complete peace and harmony for the ultimate benefit of their common country.

In the year 1926, both the work-givers and the work-takers (to use the European nomenclature) came under the direct control of a newly founded Ministry of Corporations (B. Mussolini himself acting as the Minister) and the Charter of Labor, engraved in golden letters upon the walls of the building which serves as his headquarters, tells the laboring man in minute detail everything he is supposed to do and to refrain from doing in the daily pursuit of his useful tasks.

This Golden Law starts out with the bold declaration that "Work is a social duty," and if this is true (and Signor Mussolini will tell you that it is), then it follows quite logically that a strike becomes an offense against this "social duty" and is therefore an act of high treason against the safety of the State.

However, all that, we must remember again, belongs strictly to the internal affairs of the Italian kingdom and therefore it is none of our business. Except that we over here can learn a great many useful lessons from what has happened over there in Italy.

These drastic Italian laws, strictly regulating the behavior of labor, were the direct outcome of an insufferable reign of terror and injustice on the part of the unions. The leaders of the uprisings of the years 1918 and 1919 were extremely shortsighted and thought only of their own interests. At first welcomed by all good citizens, they soon made themselves so thoroughly unpopular that these same good citizens became their sworn enemies. Thereupon labor lost everything it had just gained and was worse off than before. I recommend this unhappy chapter to the attention of Messrs. Lewis and Green. Being myself the president of an organization which is a sort of polite literary labor union, I hope that they will accept my remarks in the spirit in which they are given.

As I have probably made entirely clear by now, I feel convinced that our own democracy, if it wants to save itself and retain its self-respect, will soon have to prepare for a costly and long-drawn-out battle with the autocracies of Europe and Asia. I do not believe however that Italy, although it is an autocratically ruled country, will prove to be a major peril to our own safety. For Mussolini, even after these many years of playing the role of Caesar Augustus, is still at heart a member of his old profession and once a newspaperman, always a newspaperman, as the late and lamented James Huneker used to say, although he did not express himself quite so elegantly.

Mussolini, from the many years during which he tried to influence people by means of the spoken and written word, got a sound training in everyday human psychology. His methods since his rise to power are most certainly not the sort of methods that would be a success in our own country, but Americans are not Italians and therefore what is acceptable to them is in no way acceptable to us. The sort of oratory which in Rome will drive the people to a frenzy of enthusiasm would in New York be greeted with loud catcalls and a cordial invitation to the speaker to go jump into the nearest lake. In spite of all this Il Duce, until he joined up with Adolf Hitler, does not seem to have lost that direct and useful contact with his subjects which used to make them love him even when at times he changed them from factory fodder into gun-fodder and sent them forth to fight his wars in Africa and Spain without ever consulting them about their own wishes.

But this is now rapidly changing. During the last six months we have begun to hear of rumblings and grum-blings among the Italian working classes, though the average Italian (whether he wears a black shirt or a blue one or has no shirt at all) is still thoroughly loyal to his Big Boss. He may criticize the Duce for this or that and may occasionally groan under an almost un-bearable burden of taxation, but up to date he has shown no very noticeable desire to go back to the good old days when parliament debated, when politicians stole the money meant for national defense, and when an "Eytalian" was supposed to be all right as long as he knew his place, which was out in the fields some-where, digging ditches, or underneath the ground, boring tunnels.

A reasonable amount of self-respect is after all a good thing for the human soul and now for the first time in many centuries the Italian in Italy is able to partake of this uncustomary luxury. And as long as he is willing to shout himself hoarse for his beloved Duce, we have no reason for complaint, provided he sticks to the Piazza di Spagna in Rome to give expression to his emotions and does not use Columbus Circle in New York City for a similar purpose.

Finally—and this is also a feather in Signor Musso-lini's cap which we gratefully bestow upon him—he has rather carefully lived up to his promise that he did not intend to make Fascism an article of export. That same rule in regard to Nazism has also been pro-claimed from the roofs of the Nuremberg houses by the different leaders of Germany's foreign policy and even by Herr Hitler himself. But we know by now, especially after the recent spy trials in our country, what such Nazi promises are worth. Less than the ink it costs to print them in their subsidized newspapers. We can therefore still deal on a reasonable basis of common decency with the Italian dictator. He may, as many people believe, have a secret ambition to re-establish the old Roman Empire along the shores of the Mediterranean. Let those who live there fight it out with him. We need our power to combat the man who hopes to turn the Atlantic Ocean into a *mare germanicum*—a sort of large German inland sea—and if we are wise, we shall hasten to do so before the day has come when our navy must rudely remind Berlin of the existence of the Monroe Doctrine.

Recently neutral observers have noticed with con-siderable astonishment that Mussolini seems to be los-ing his grip, that he is no longer as certain of himself as he used to be, that he is beginning to make techni-cal mistakes which show that he is no longer quite sure of himself. That mighty demagogue with the imperial frown ("Duce! Duce! Duce!") now looks worried. Occasionally he loses his cue, and his old "routine" lacks some of the brilliant qualities which

were so characteristic of him in the older days. He
now has to work for his effects and he has been observed watching the gallery to see whether perhaps a
few of the patrons are not walking out on him. He
never used to do this. Like Harry Lauder, he only
needed to walk out on the stage to have the public
welcome him with never-ending ovations.

The reason for this, it seems to me, is as plain as
the light of day. Mussolini's Italian audiences do not
like the German comedy stuff that recently has been
introduced into that old Italian act with which they
were familiar and which they loved. The appearance
of a group of Nazi yodelers immediately after a glam-
orous scene in the moonlit Colosseum and a taran-
tella danced in dirndl costume can never be popular
in a country which loves its Donizetti and its Verdi
straight and which, within the realm of the theater,
has always remained faithful to its native *commedia
dell' arte*. Of course, since the star is also his own
stage manager and the sole proprietor of the theater,
no one feels any particular urge to criticize the performance or to show signs of boredom and downright
disapproval. And as all the newspapers in the country
are controlled by this modern Salvini, there really is no
chance of telling him that his most recent appear-
ances have failed to give satisfaction. But we have
it upon excellent authority that the leaders of the
"claque" (the manipulators of the organized applause
in all European theaters and in the Metropolitan
Opera House of New York) recently took their courage in both hands and discreetly informed the star
that something very serious was the matter with his

show and that it was getting more and more difficult
to assure their hero of his customary *evivas* and cur-
tain calls.

Being an old newspaper scribe with a fine sense of
public opinion, Signor Mussolini can no longer be in
any doubt about what has happened to him since he
went into partnership with the heavy comedian from
across the Alps. Once having signed this disastrous
contract, he may not, for the moment at least, know
how to extricate himself from his awkward position.
But perhaps we could help him a little.

It was the (to us) incredible policy of England's
Foreign Office just before the beginning of the Ethi-
opian adventure which drove Italy into the arms of
Nazi Germany. But the same people who refused to
combine forces with our own Mr. Stimson, when in
the year 1931, he suggested that Japan be not allowed
to break her solemn promises in regard to China,
these same panic-stricken British reactionaries, completely blinded by their fears of Russia, are still in
power in London. Therefore, the sooner we recognize
that we can no longer depend upon the English to
stand by our side in our fight for democracy, the better it will be for all of us on this side of the ocean.
It will not be easy to accustom ourselves to a world
in which the word of England counts for no more
than the word of one of the Central American Republics, but such is the case. From now on, we will
have to formulate our own foreign policies and we
must accept our new role as the protector of the ideals
of democracy or see that form of government disap-

pear altogether from the face of the earth. Under those circumstances, one of the first things we should do is to consider the possibilities of encouraging an open break between Italy and Germany.

The alliance between these two nations is both un-natural and unpopular. The personalities of the dictators who rule over these countries are in complete contrast with each other. Their subjects, too, have nothing in common. They find themselves bedfellows because outside influences have pushed them into the same couch, which is probably the worst of all possible reasons to share any sort of a mattress.

What concrete measures we should take to break up the famous "axis" between Berlin and Rome—that I do not know, and if I did, I would be most careful not to mention it, for I too am a member of Signor Mussolini's former profession. I am a newspaperman and not a diplomat, but it surely will take no Talleyrand or Bismarck to show us how it ought to be done and how it can be done.

The Führer is the biographer's friend. He makes it easy for us to write about him. The Mussolinis and the Stalins and all the other dictators, both of the major and minor leagues, force us to guess at their motives by wrapping themselves up in a dark cloak of literary anonymity and by only revealing their innermost thoughts very occasionally when they have got drunk on their own eloquence or are so mad that they no longer know what they are saying.

Not so Adolf Hitler. He has told us all there is to

know (and a great deal more) in his shotgun best seller, which bears the name of *Mein Kampf* or *My Battle*.

In case you want to read this remarkable document for yourself, you will first of all have to learn German. There is an English version, published in Boston by the admirable house of Houghton Mifflin, but quite worthless, as the translator has not only rendered it into the American vernacular but also (according to the title page) has done considerable "abridging." That is always a dangerous business, that business of abridging historical documents. For that sort of abridgment is usually a deliberate form of "editing" and editing for a very definite purpose.

For more than half a century now the world at large has seriously condemned the way Bismarck had abridged the famous Ems dispatch so that from a mere harmless statement of fact it became a fighting issue between Germany and France. The German historians have of course tried to defend the conduct of their Iron Chancellor by stating that after all, "he only left out a few words." That was it! By "leaving out a few words," any clever editor can turn the Ten Commandments into a direct appeal for sin and vice. And by leaving out all those blatant and puerile vilifications of France and England and of the democratic form of government at large, which make this book so interesting to the student of abnormal psychology, the publishers have made this American version of Hitler's *My Battle* into something that is about as reliable as the prospectus of a company trying to make gold out of sea water or of a political party offering to pay each one of us thirty dollars a week for the rest of our natural lives without any noticeable increase in taxation.

However, together with most of the rest of the world, I have long since discovered that the word "ethics" has no place in those German lexicons, revised according to the gospel of the eminent Dr. Goebbels. So I shall now drop the matter, after giving the reader a delicate hint about the reliability of this Anglo-Saxon version of Adolf Hitler's *Mein Kampf* and suggesting that he partake of it not only with a bit of salt but with a liberal dose of bicarbonate of soda.

The original volume in its original version (the later German editions too have been dangerously mutilated) is one of the most extraordinary historical documents of all time. It combines the naïveté of the late Jean-Jacques Rousseau (the exploiter of the confessional style of literature) with the frenzied wrath of an Old Testament prophet. And in between these violent rhapsodies and fulminations, we come occasionally upon high-sounding historical disquisitions which, if you ever happen to have taught school, will remind you, with a sudden catch of the breath, of those delightful cabalistic examination papers in History 1 that were written by some of your less intelligent Freshmen, desperately in need of a pass mark but not having the slightest idea of what they were talking about.

Of course, this sort of criticism is not entirely fair. The friends of the Führer may well answer me, "Yes, and what of it? After all, Hitler is not a professional historian. You are. And where are you? You are sitting in a little house in Old Greenwich, picking away at a typewriter ten hours each day to pay your grocer. And where is he? In Berlin, in Prague, in London. Tomorrow perhaps he will be in Sweden or Paris or anywhere he wants to go. So what do you prove by calling him names and comparing him to your Freshmen in Cornell?"

As usual, these logical Teutons would be entirely right. Herr Hitler is today the most powerful autocrat in the entire world and he can, if he so desires, have my head cut off while I (much to my regret) can never hope to reciprocate. But just the same, it is exceedingly dangerous for the safety of all of us when a man who now has the whole of Europe at his mercy is not merely ignorant but knows an awful lot of things which are not so.

I believe that here I am borrowing from the wisdom of the late Artemus Ward. I am sure he won't mind, although he may envy me for having an opponent who would have been so completely to his own taste, a mixture of lower-middle-class respectability and pretensions of grandeur born out of a hopeless feeling of mediocrity and four dreadful years of residence among the derelicts of the Viennese slums.

"Beware of the man with a grievance!" Those words might well be writ large over the portals that lead to the study of history. According to William Congreve, "Hell hath no fury like a woman scorned." But how about the male of the species who feels that Fate has rejected him and that he has not received those rewards at the hands of his fellow men to which his natural abilities entitled him? Compared to him and his power for evil, the scorned lady is as harmless as a newborn babe. She at least can be placated. Her hysterical anger can easily be appeased by giving her a better fur coat than any of her neighbors, by taking her aside and assuring her that she has the glamour of the Garbo with the charm of little Shirley Temple. But the hysterical male—there is nothing this side of the grave that can stop him, once he has been given a chance to assert himself. Often enough he can't even be stopped after he has departed this life, and whole generations must suffer because one man, evil of heart but brilliant of brain, had thought himself belittled in his efforts and therefore wanted to get even.

I know of no more contemptible expression in the English language than these three words, "to get even." I can understand a healthy anger and I can fully sympathize with a perfectly normal desire to go forth and give a sound beating to a fellow who has done you a mean trick. I am entirely familiar with most of the lower impulses to which human flesh and blood are at times subject and which are apt to manifest themselves in very unpleasant ways. But if I were to classify the whole register of sins (big sins and little sins and 50-50 sins) I would place, way at the top of that list, that pollution of the soul which manifests itself in the wish "to get even."

For it implies a slow and smoldering sort of hatred, which will nurse and tend a private grievance until it so completely fills a person's mind that there is no room left for any of the finer impulses such as that quality of mercy which is truly said to be one of the most glorious attributes of the good Lord himself. Everything which Adolf Hitler has said and done since he started upon his present career has been a direct expression of his all-consuming ambition to revenge himself for his unhappy youth.

Poor little fellow, who had to make his Hell right here on our fair earth so that he himself might experience a few moments of relief and forget his hopeless sense of inferiority!

You remember of course how annoying it is when you see a stranger on the street and suddenly say to yourself, "That face reminds me of someone I know," and yet, for the life of you, you cannot remember whose face it is of which you are being reminded. You will spend days and weeks following up every possible clue. In the middle of the night you will wake up with that embarrassing problem disturbing your slumbers, for you are quite sure that that face looked like someone whom you had known quite intimately, but who was it?

This happened to me after I had made the acquaintance of Adolf Hitler within the pages of his book. He worried me for a long time. Had I run across him on the Forum of imperial Rome? Had I been told about him when I went to my catechism? Or (more likely) was he the reincarnation of one of those spiritual malformations so common during the Middle Ages?

Gradually I was obliged to rule all these candidates

out and I came to the conclusion that such a dwarfed personality could only have been produced under the stress of some great revolutionary movement. And I began to study the men and women who had taken a part in the social and economic upheavals of the last two thousand years, the leaders of those agrarian upheavals which did so much to hasten the downfall of the Roman Empire, of the peasants who during the sixteenth century had risen in rebellion against their cruel feudal masters and who had incited Martin Luther to the most brutal of all his utterances: "Kill them, smite them, burn them, hang them, break them on the wheel!" and other ravings of a person completely frightened out of his wits. Often I had, for a moment at least, felt that I had got him, that at last I had found the man I was looking for, but although often there were certain similarities, there were also marked dissimilarities. And then one day I knew! An unhealthy face, bearing the ghastly imprint of a most complete lack of inner harmony, sneered at me from a little paper-covered volume in my library and the creature lifted a threatening finger while his thin lips whispered an ominous "Beware!" And behold! Maximilian Robespierre slipped into my room.

Once upon a time I decided that I would write a sequel to my *Rembrandt* and that I would try to describe the whole of the eighteenth century as in *R.v.R.* I had tried to give a full-length picture of the period between the years 1600 and 1670. I had thereupon collected quite a number of books upon the revolutionary era in France and I had gathered together everything I could find that had any bearing on the Great Incorruptible, the never-sufficiently-to-be-despised Maximilian Robespierre. That is how I happened to have that little paper-covered booklet in my workshop, but when I picked it up, I was struck by something which years before I had written on the cover. It was but one single word and the word was "hysteria."

Underneath it I read a hastily scrawled reference to a certain volume and a certain page in the Encyclopædia Britannica. I had forgotten what that article said. I reread it and with the permission of the editors of that ancient and honorable publication I shall now reprint it in full, for it is a complete and detailed diagnosis of the case of Adolf Hitler, the most dangerous hysterical patient since that morning when, amidst the derisive howls and catcalls of his former dupes, the mutilated body of the great apostle of self-righteous rectitude was pushed underneath the knife of the guillotine and Maximilian Robespierre bade farewell to a world that had meant nothing to him but a cosmic chance to get even.

Here is that article in question. Even in its abbreviated form, it is rather long but it is tremendously important if you really want to understand the dictator who today is our most dangerous enemy and whom we will have to fight ere long, if we care to maintain the good right of a free people to rule itself according to its own desires. I am now quoting from page 27 of volume 12 of the Encyclopædia Britannica, 14th edition, and my thanks to the editors for their generous co-operation.

HYSTERIA, a term applied to a mental affection which occurs usually in individuals of neurotic and unstable constitutions. It is manifested by an undue susceptibility to external impressions, emotional episodes, and marked sensory, psychic and motor disturbance. Though classed among so-called "nervous" diseases, it is functional in origin, and no organic change in the nervous system is known to exist. Physicians of the past supposed that hysteria occurred only in women and resulted from a wandering of the uterus or womb; hence its name; but after the experiences of the World War it has been more and more clearly realized that men may be as much affected as women.

Though heredity has a definite influence, modern knowledge has shown that environmental factors in early life and faulty education are of main importance. . . .
. . . Various other theories of such mental dissociation have been formulated and the most important and interpretative is that of Sigmund Freud of Vienna. [Now of London. Ed.] According to this worker, the hysterical symptom is the result of a conflict between the personality and some "wish" which is out of harmony with the personal ego, and is therefore repressed. The repression, however, is not entirely successful, and the wish in the unconscious mind, being dynamic, forces its way into consciousness in a symbolic and disguised form. The symptom is thus a compromise between the two urges at play. . . .

The symptoms of hysteria are manifold and complex and may appear in many combinations. They may be physical or mental. Among the former we may note paralysis of limbs, spasms of muscles, tremors, loss of voice or speech, loss of sensation in the skin, blindness, vomiting, etc. . . . There are, however, points of differentiation which careful investigation will usually reveal. The mental symptoms can all be looked upon as the result of the independent functioning of a dissociated part of the content of the mind. The chief are memory gaps, sleepwalking, fugues (wandering attacks of which there is no subsequent recollection), trances, hallucinations, deliria, and dream states. Double personality would be explained on a similar basis. In such a condition the split-off mental functions are so extensive that a second complete personality is formed. Freud classifies hysteria into two forms—conversion hysteria, when the psychic excitation is converted into some bodily innervation, and anxiety hysteria, when the symptoms are purely mental. In the latter category are included those cases evidencing anxiety, depression and morbid fears. In the minor form of hysteria the individual tends to be nervous and excitable, show exaggerated emotion, lack of control, with a liability to phantasy, egoism, and craving for attention and sympathy. . . .

For the sake of brevity I have omitted a few sentences from this excellent summing up. I have however been most careful not to "edit" this article in any way, as you may see for yourself by comparing it with the original.

And now let us study the case of Adolf Hitler, as he tells it to us himself in the original German edition of his book, My Battle, that you, the reader, can form your own judgment and see in how far you agree or disagree with my diagnosis.

Here it may be better to follow the example of old Plutarch and study our patient together with a fellow sufferer, so as to have a more complete chance of bringing out the salient points in the characters of both men. And, of course, there is only one suitable candidate for this doubtful honor and that is Maximilian Robespierre.

Well then, in the first place, both Hitler and Robespierre started life under a cloud. It need not have been a cloud, for other people have survived certain irregularities in their immediate past without being any the worse for them. But such reactions depend entirely upon the character of the person in question. There are girls who never quite recover from the shock of having been kissed on the tip of the nose by some overardent swain, taking them home from a church social. And there are others who can gaily live through half a dozen love affairs and then marry and become the best of mothers and wives without the slightest qualms about their somewhat irregular past.

Unfortunately for themselves, neither Hitler nor Robespierre was that sort of a girl. They were what one might call "brooders." Being unattractive personalities and unpopular among their fellow classmates and never smiled upon by any of the members of the opposite sex, they were magnificent examples of what modern psychology, I believe, calls "introverts," people who divert all their thoughts within themselves with the energy of a horse swallowing air. Not being a veterinary, I do not know whether such a horse finally expires as the result of a gastric explosion. He might. But the mind, not being made of the same material substance as the horse's belly, such an explosion (which, unless it killed the patient, would give him considerable relief) does not behave in such a rational fashion and the psychological swallowing process continues until the patient dies a natural or violent death. In the meantime, his brain has become a cesspool of imaginary slights and imaginary insults and very real frustrations and the poor devil suffers tortures of which we normal people cannot possibly form any conception. But we are bound to take cognizance of the existence of this spiritual sewer in those of our neighbors thus afflicted, for like its physical namesake, the spiritual cloaca will fill the entire atmosphere for miles around with its unsavory and poisonous exhalations.

Both Hitler and Robespierre were issue of a family that suffered from a sort of inner restlessness which is often found among people who could never quite adjust themselves to their original surroundings. That part of Austria in which Hitler's father and mother were born was far from prosperous. Incessant labor alone could save these little peasants from starvation and small wonder that Hitler's father made almost herculean efforts to escape from such a life of bondage and to attain a modicum of comfort and safety by passing those (to him) rigorous examinations which would allow him to spend the rest of his days as a full-fledged Imperial and Royal Apostolic official, with a right to a pension after so many years of faithful service.

It never was much of a job, being merely a minor variety of customs inspectorship, but to old Alois Schicklgruber it represented the fulfillment of a lifelong dream. He could now wear the double-headed eagle of Austria on the buttons of his uniform and, best of all, he was entitled to a pension. One does not readily call a man who wears the double-headed eagle of the Emperor on the buttons of his uniform and who is entitled to a pension, a bastard. One politely says, "Good morning, Herr Amtsassistent," and humbly touches one's cap.

In regard to fathers, Robespierre was much worse off than Hitler. For only a hasty marriage had prevented little Maximilian from having been born out of wedlock, and after a short and futile attempt to take care of his rapidly increasing family, François de Robespierre gave up the attempt altogether. He disappeared from view, never to be heard of again, and left Maximilian and his brother and sisters to the mercies of their relatives.

As for the mothers of these two sad heroes, they were shadowy figures and we shall probably never perceive them very clearly. The mother of Maximilian was the daughter of an obscure innkeeper in the city of Arras and the mother of Adolf (her husband's third and last wife) belonged to the impoverished line of a family of smalltime farmers.

I am not giving you these details for the sake of a little backstairs gossip. In America we can still honor a man for what he has made of himself, and all the more credit and honor to him for having risen above his earlier surroundings. But I must repeat what I said a moment ago—it was not what had actually happened to them that interests us here but the influence of these events upon the characters of our two heroes.

Arras (like Noyon, the birthplace of the austere and morose John Calvin) was situated in that northern

plain of France where the landscape is without any
grace or charm, where it always seems to be raining
and where the people have no means of relief from
the dreary melancholy of their dull daily lives except
applejack and scandalmongering. The relatives of
Maximilian, especially his pious and devoted aunts,
were people of considerable importance in their own
little social circle, for Arras, which for centuries had
been under Spanish domination, was a town domi-
nated by the priesthood and such stanch pillars of the
church as the Demoiselles de Robespierre were not to
be taken lightly or to be treated with disrespect. Nevertheless, Maximilian, forever shuttled between his
plebeian grandfather, the tavern keeper, and his genteel
aunts, suffered profound agonies of shame and humili-
ation, which left their mark upon his entire attitude
toward life. And these unfortunate family affairs em-
bittered him until he felt that he was a being with a
righteous grievance and must somehow get even or
commit suicide.

As for Adolf, he had never known his father's first
wife, who had been fourteen years older than her husband and such a perpetual invalid that her husband
finally had obtained a "separation" from her, as di-
vorce in clerical Austria was an impossibility. Neither
had he ever seen his father's second wife, who had
been a cook in the Schicklgruber household and had
borne old Alois a son (afterwards legitimized) while
the first wife was still alive. But he must have heard
many rumors about his father's irregular birth and his
equally irregular ménage from his schoolmates. For
children are experts at inflicting pain, and as a result

of their malice this son of an old man (Alois was fifty-two when Adolf was born and fifty-seven when his last child saw the light of day), who was a hypersensitive child with a veritable genius for self-pity, did the only thing he could do under the circumstances. He declared war upon society, when most other boys are thinking of going fishing or kissing the hired man's daughter behind the barn.

A sense of frustration—a self-imposed frustration, but nevertheless a most unhealthy emotion in creatures quite so young—accompanied both our heroes through the entire period of their adolescence.

Robespierre, a very bright lad with an excellent if pompous brain, enjoyed a much better education than Adolf. The Church took him in hand (at the request of the well-to-do aunts) and after he had learned all the local parochial schools could teach him, he was sent to Paris to the famous College of Louis le Grand. There an incident occurred which put its mark upon the entire further development of his character.

Ambition was the besetting sin of the son of François de Robespierre. He felt himself to be predestined for great things. But he was a charity boy who in his shabby coat had to stand by and watch when his more fortunate playmates, His Highness, the Prince de Rohan-Chabot or His Grace, the Duke of Montmorency, were called for in their fathers' carriages to spend the holidays among the luxuries of the ancestral castle. He saw them go in all their silks and satins, a little sword dangling from their side, but he, the outcast, had to remain behind and spend the endless months of summer in the lonely halls of his boarding school, for the trip home was too expensive. It was torture, plain, unadulterated torture, for a boy of his make-up. So he got even with his comrades by being brighter than they were, by studying his lessons harder than they cared to do, by getting higher marks. That is to say, he thought that he got even, but all he did was to establish for himself the reputation of an insufferable bore and prig. He never realized it but the others despised him for those very qualities which, in his own eyes, were manifestations of shining virtue.

But every dog has his day and little Maximilian too was to enjoy a brief hour of glory. For the first time in almost a hundred years, the college was to be honored by a visit from royalty and the cleverest boy of all was to be the official spokesman for both the faculty and the students. Maximilian was that cleverest boy. The authorities gave him a beautiful new suit of clothes (the first really decent clothes he had ever had) and they rehearsed him carefully in the piece he would have to recite.

Now of course he should have been contented, but he was not. Again he had reason to feel himself slighted. In the year 1674, when the college had entertained royalty for the last time, the valedictorian (as we would call him) had been garbed in a "patrician costume." Maximilian knew this because he always knew everything. His raiment was quite resplendent, but the coat was not of a "patrician cut." That, of course, had been done for the express purpose of humiliating him in the eyes of his richer fellow students. And then (and this was really pathetic!) on the morning of the great day it rained. It rained, of course, to spoil his success. Next the royal party was half an hour late and that undoubtedly was part of a plot to crush the sagging spirits of the most deserving of all the pupils of the College of Louis le Grand.

But that was only a beginning. Worse was to follow to make this the most horrible day in the poor infant's life.

The Queen, who like all sensible women, hated to get wet when she was expected to look her best, suggested to her husband that they cut this visit to the school as short as possible and not even leave their carriage. Louis said yes. He would always say yes, until the day his beautiful wife was to suggest a course of folly that was to lead both of them to the scaffold.

The school authorities humbly requested that their Majesties at least graciously deign to listen to the ode of welcome to be pronounced by young Monsieur de Robespierre. Their Majesties most graciously deigned to do so and now behold our poor, shivering Maximilian, so sure of his lines but so uncertain in his deportment, obliged to kneel down in the mud of the street with the rain pouring down his neck, reciting his hexameters which (as he felt firmly convinced) were infinitely better than His Majesty himself could ever hope to write. And then see him hastening back to his forlorn abode just underneath the roof, his knees covered with dirt, his coat ruined, his hair straggling down his forehead, and worst of all, the King had not even looked at him nor had he told him what a fine fellow he was and how clever of him to write such wonderful Latin verses.

A mere coincidence, you will say—an event of no importance whatsoever. Yes, if it had happened to you or to me. But it happened to Maximilian de Robespierre. In his case, there were no events without any importance. Everything that happened either flattered his ego or it belittled his pretentions toward greatness. When that happened, he could nurse a grudge longer and more bitterly than anybody else. Until the day Hitler was born!

Now let us for a moment study the career of Adolf Hitler during the most impressionable years of his life. You will be struck by the similarity between his earlier existence and that of Robespierre.

Adolf Hitler, too, did not care for his home. He also detested his father but most of all he hated himself. For what was there about himself that he could have liked? He was not an attractive-looking boy. He belonged to an obscure family in an obscure corner of a country he despised, as it did not live up to his ideals of a glorious Teutonic empire, a sort of perpetual *Nibelungenlied* with music by Richard Wagner and little Adolf in the role of Siegfried.

But as he had neither money nor any sort of social position, his future promised to be as uninteresting and drab as the past of most of his ancestors, and there was nothing to do, therefore, but to make his escape and try his luck elsewhere. Once he had achieved fame and glory, he would return to let himself be admired and envied by his neighbors, but until then they would see and hear nothing of him.

He certainly lived up to this program. The day after

his armies had occupied Austria, he was back in his native village and did everything that was expected of a native son who had made good. He went to the cemetery and visited the dear old cottage where he had learned to prattle his earliest prayers at the knee of his mother while old Alois was waiting outside for him with a switch to cure him of his fool notions about wanting to become an "art-artist."

Adolf Hitler was fourteen years old when his father died. During all that time he had apparently had only one ambition—to become an artist. But whenever the son mentioned the word "artist," the father grew red in the face and flew into a green rage. What! the child of a respectable imperial customhouse official wearing long hair and wasting his time smearing daubs of paint on pieces of canvas in some unsavory garret? And that, after he, the father, had made every possible sacrifice to attain his present distinguished position, with the right to a lifelong pension! Never! He would rather see him dead!

One rarely argued about one's future with a father of that type. One either said yes, or one said nothing at all and did as one pleased. Adolf Hitler followed the latter course. At the age of twelve he became an intellectual syndicalist and began to indulge in acts of sabotage. He went patiently enough to the village school but he refused to exert himself. Except for two subjects, freehand drawing and gymnastics, his marks became even worse than they had been before. He also took a casual interest in geography and history, chiefly because he liked the teacher who handled these subjects, but everything else he completely neglected. And, being indifferent to corporal chastisement or any other form of punishment, little Adolf blithely went his way and quite naturally used up his vast reservoirs of spare energy in making himself the leader of every movement that threatened to upset the discipline of the school. For he was born to be the leader of a gang. Undoubtedly he will die that way too.

Then he discovered the theater, and from then on it was possible to escape from all unpleasant realities of life by associating one's self with the characters on the stage. Schiller and Richard Wagner revealed unto him a world of which he had never suspected. At the same time, in the parental attic, he unearthed a history of the war of 1870, filled with beautiful pictures and glorious memories of Germany's victories over France. But alas, he was an Austrian and not a German and therefore all that greatness could mean nothing to him. But his history teacher, an ardent advocate of the Pan-German ideal, consoled him. "The day will come," so this honest pedagogue prophesied, "that all of us, of German descent, will once more belong to one mighty Teutonic nation that will stretch from the Mediterranean to the Baltic, just like the Empire of the Middle Ages, and that will stand supreme among the peoples of this earth."

Little Adolf listened with bated breath. Here at last was a role worthy of his own ambitions. Such a task would need another Charlemagne, and he felt himself to be his logical successor.

Unfortunately, just then his health gave out. He

was threatened with a weakness of the lungs. At times
he lost the use of his voice. Some doctors went so far
as to predict that he would die an early death. They
seem to have mistaken symptoms of hysteria for manifestations of tuberculosis.

Meanwhile the future Führer was getting nowhere
at all with his studies. He had a good brain but he
lacked self-discipline and his mind was not on his
work. His father was dead. His mother had little control over him. And so he went his own sweet way and
did pretty much as he liked and in October of the
year 1907 he moved to Vienna to prepare himself for
the Imperial Academy of Art. In order to enter, he
must pass a preliminary examination which included a
piece of freehand drawing. He failed. Half a year later,
he once more presented himself. He failed even worse
than before and the examining board considered him
to be so completely lacking in any original talent that
they refused to let him try again.

The road toward fame by way of the Garden of the
Muses was definitely closed. Adolf went home to hide
his shame and to take care of his mother, who was in
the last stages of tuberculosis. In December of the
year 1908 she went to her final reward. Her son Adolf
remained behind, a complete and hopeless failure. He
was just nineteen years old.

Then follows the most decisive period in his life,
those four long years of abject misery spent in the
slums of Vienna. Still wearing the clothes and still
speaking the vernacular which indicate his slightly

more genteel antecedents, he now becomes an inhabit-
ant of those municipal and private flophouses where
one can get a bed for a few pennies a night and where
one must tuck one's shoes underneath the pillow for
fear that otherwise they may be gone in the morning.

During these four years of horror, the legend arose
of the "Austrian paper hanger." That legend is a myth.
Respectable paper hangers belong to a union, and
this crusader for a rejuvenated Germany, this dreamer
of Teutonic glory, hated and despised all labor unions.
The Knights of the Holy Grail and Hagen's mighty
warriors had not carried union cards. Neither, therefore, would he. A thousand times no! Rather would he
starve. And starve he did, unless he had luck and made
a few pennies turning out "hand-painted" postal cards
which a friend with a commercial soul (not therefore
a Knight of the Holy Grail) was willing to peddle
among the cheaper shops of the suburbs, where the
owners of small butcher stores and one-chair barber
shops would buy them for their wives, to delight these
simple souls with a piece of real art.

Often when he could not get hold of the few gro-
schen necessary for a bed in a public shelter, he would
spend the night on a bench in the park. Whenever the
art business picked up a little, he could return to his
municipal boardinghouse, happy to enjoy the warmth
of a single thin woolen cover, and to be protected
against the rain. In the morning, charitable monks
would provide him and his fellow sufferers with a bowl
of hot soup. In the evening, someone luckier than
himself would perhaps throw him a chunk of stale
bread or a piece of sausage made of horse meat.

His clothes grew so shabby that he could hardly wear them. When winter came, he tried his hand at snow-shoveling, but his leaky shoes and his lack of physical strength made this sort of work an unendurable torture. Or he tried to make a few pennies as a porter at the railroad station. But invariably in the end he was obliged to return to that asylum in Meidling, founded and maintained by a Jewish philanthropist.

Others have gone through similar experiences. In case they survived (as a great many have done) and returned to a normal existence, they were apt to have learned the meaning of the words compassion and pity. Not so Adolf Hitler. By a strange alchemy of the soul, all such experiences in his case were immediately converted into bitterness and hatred. For his all-consuming ego would never allow him to confess that he himself might be partly responsible for his failures. It was all the fault of obscure and malicious outside influences which conspired to keep him down because he was the prophet of a new day when the German people, reborn in the spirit (his own spirit), would march forth to carry their ideals of Teutonic perfection unto the very ends of the world.

This is not a piece of mere conjecture on the part of the author of this book. All those who knew him during these dreadful years agree that his mind was forever dwelling upon problems which to most of his comrades seemed just so much moonshine. What did they care about abstract political problems while they were on the brink of starvation? Why all this nonsense about the destinies of a fatherland that meant nothing to them? They occasionally listened to him, for he was forever talking, talking and talking, and it was hard to get away, once he had started. But not one of his listeners was willing to take the poor fellow seriously, this John the Baptist in his ridiculous frock coat, a hand-me-down which for many years was his only garment and which, together with his pale and emaciated face, made him look like a scarecrow. No one except Adolf Hitler.

You will remember what Mirabeau had said about Robespierre. "Watch out for that young man! He actually believes everything he says!" Alas! in the case of the Führer there was no Mirabeau to give us that warning.

Adolf Hitler came to hate Vienna with a bitter and relentless hatred. Old-fashioned Viennese are apt to explain this feeling by the fact that Adolf always remained a *Spiessbürger*—a small small-town citizen, who was not able to change himself into a real cosmopolitan after the pattern of the easygoing and gracious inhabitants of that city where the people since centuries had learned to exist on a plan of "live and let live."

A strange hodgepodge of all sorts of nationalities, it had long since learned that only a complete willingness to give and take would enable it to exist without a perpetual state of civil war. For the realm of the Habsburgs resembled a boardinghouse on the lower East Side of New York.

Until the end of the eighteenth century, Spanish had remained the official language of the court. German had then gradually replaced it but Italian had been quite as common as German. After the Hungarian rebellion of 1848, the rulers had also been obliged to learn Magyar. When Hitler starved in his garret, there even was an heir to the throne who by preference spoke a Slavic tongue because he had married a beautiful lady of Czech origin. Not to forget all sorts of strange dialects from the Balkans and the Carpathian Mountains and that peculiar intonation of the voice which betrayed the speaker as being of Jewish origin.

Yes, in this one particular respect, the Habsburgs were very much like the Lord Almighty—they, too, harbored some very strange customers, although on the whole they kept them in better order than their heavenly colleagues. And out of this hopeless mixture of races and ethnological leftovers, they had actually succeeded in making a state which in turn had given birth to a state of mind, which we have got to call Austrian because we cannot possibly classify it as anything else.

For half a thousand years Vienna had been the center of this purely Austrian culture, which bestowed so many blessings upon us. Is it necessary to give you any names? Try and imagine what our music and our theater and our art would have been without Vienna and without those artists who had worked within the shadow of the imperial court. Compared to the capital of this hybrid empire, Berlin always remained a third-rate provincial nest. Paris came nearest to being its rival, except within the field of music. Rome lived almost entirely on the memory of its former glories.

Florence might have outrivaled Vienna if it had not perished as a result of its everlasting political strife. As for London, it was rich but crude and beefy, compared to the gay city on the far from blue Danube, where one drank *Heuriger* instead of whisky and ate *Kaisertorte* instead of green and pink pieces of pastry. In short, Vienna was more than a national capital. It, too, was a state of mind and gave us one of the most delightful developments of the human spirit of the last five hundred years.

But of all this, Adolf Hitler remained as completely ignorant as if he had never set foot in the Kärtnerstrasse. The spirit of Vienna filled him with disgust. It was too easygoing, it was too spontaneous, it had too much gaiety and lacked all force, all discipline, all those barrack virtues which he admired so immensely in his Prussian neighbors. And worst of all, it was full of grace. This the graceless one could never forgive. He has had his revenge. Vienna is gone, and gone for good. It has become a depot for Nazi recruits.

There are many volumes which will give you the details of the Führer's existence while he was living the life of what, in our crude democracy, we would call "the life of a bum." I need not repeat them here for that is not the purpose of this book. I must however draw your attention to the development of one of the most dangerous obsessions which since then has influenced all the acts of this poor psychopathic patient and which first of all began to manifest itself during those four years spent among the derelicts and outcasts of the Austrian capital. I refer of course to his phobia in regard to the Jews.

This is really a very curious development, for during his years at home, Hitler had never come in contact with those anti-Semitic prejudices which are as old as the Jewish people themselves and which are the result of a great many different factors of which I can only mention the more important ones.

In the first place, the Jews are Orientals, forced since time immemorial to live among people with a completely different religious and cultural background. When times are prosperous, these differences do not play much of a role, but when times are hard, they become more accentuated and then they are a cause of serious danger. For the bartering habits of the old bazaar have closely stuck to a great many members of this tribe of natural-born merchants. Also, since they have no country of their own, they are much more internationally minded than the people among whom they live, and, having relatives or connections in every land, they enjoy the advantages of those intimate cosmopolitan ramifications which are of such tremendous benefit to trade that our big manufacturing companies will spend millions to develop them artificially. This had a tendency to give the Jews a quicker power of recuperation than those who knew nobody outside of their own frontiers. For until the rise to power of Adolf Hitler it had never happened that all of the people everywhere were persecuting all of the Jews at exactly the same time and so the victims usually had some place where they could go and begin life anew.

But there is one more aspect of this terribly difficult and hopelessly complicated problem which one rarely hears mentioned in connection with the Jewish race but which seems to me to be of far-reaching importance. The Jew in many subtle ways is undoubtedly slightly different from those around him, but he suffers because he is not quite different enough. If he were a Negro or had the slanting eyes of the Chinese, everybody would take it for granted that he was not entirely like himself and would make allowances. But the Jew is *almost* like the Christian (using both terms in a very wide and vague sense) and yet he is not *quite* like the Christian. And that is very irritating to a great many people who seem to resent nothing as much as that others can't or won't be completely like them themselves.

The opinions I am offering here are entirely theoretical and the Führer is a man of action, and not in the least interested in theory. Also he loves strong effects and brilliant contrasts, and delicate shadings of colors are never found on the palette of this retired artist. Therefore he likes his anti-Semitism straight, like the addicts of bathtub gin during the days of the Noble Experiment who refused to touch anything that did not burn out the lining of their stomachs and who were forever denouncing their more moderate brethren as weaklings and sissies.

Remains the question when and where and under what circumstances had Adolf Hitler acquired the taste for this kind of poison. It almost looks as if he had come upon it by accident, for during a great many

years, before he proclaimed his crusade against the In-
fidel, he had been experimenting with all sorts of sub-
stitutes, with anti-Catholicism and anti-Protestantism
and even with anti-Christianism and of course with
anti-Democratism. Some of these *Ersatz* articles were
fairly successful, but the good old anti-Semitic slogans,
having been already on the market for centuries past,
and the Jews not being a people very apt to answer
violence with violence, he found it on the whole easier
and also more profitable to stick to the tried and true
formula of "Kill the Jew!" than to invent some new
rabble-rousing concoction of his own.

Some day we shall perhaps know the real secret of
this anti-Jewish obsession which Adolf Hitler, to the
everlasting disgrace of both himself and his followers,
has turned into one of the Articles of Faith of the
new German creed. But until that moment comes, we
can only guess at the reason. We must however accept the fact as he will have to accept the consequences.

These consequences have been disastrous in the ex-
treme. They have brought dishonor upon the German
name. They have given large numbers of people of
very inferior qualities a chance to avenge their own
sense of defeat upon their brighter neighbors who had
no adequate means of defense. An easy victory is apt
to brutalize the victor. It is doing so at a frightening
rate of speed in a rapidly increasing number of countries. The blame for this rests squarely upon the shoulders of Adolf Hitler, Führer of the Third German
Reich.

The Great War put an end to Hitler's career as a social outcast. In May of 1913 he had left Vienna for
Munich, where he now tried to make a living drawing
commercial posters. A chance acquaintance who had
picked him up just when he was being evicted for the
nonpayment of his rent allowed him to sleep on the
sofa in his own bedroom. The strange fellow boarder
did not abuse his privileges. As always he lived a solitary existence, rigorously avoiding any sort of direct
contact with those who had made this Bavarian town
a famous center of music and art. But when he found
that a few people in some near-by beer garden were
willing to listen to his endless political harangues, he
was ready to oblige, and his rhetorical improvisation
did not come to an end until his hearers had either
paid for his beer or had gone home.

But at last he had his opportunity. War was declared. The German people rushed to arms. Hitler,
who had avoided doing his military service in his own
country (the Austrian police had never been able to
locate him), now offered himself as a volunteer to the
recruiting officers of the Sixteenth Bavarian Reserve
Infantry Regiment. In those first days after the outbreak of hostilities, no one bothered much about cre-
dentials. Hitler was accepted and the next four years
he spent on the western front.

We have very few reliable details about Adolf's
career as a soldier. We know that he survived. We
know that he got the Iron Cross—First Class—during
one of the last months of the war. We know that he
loved this life which demanded "blind obedience to

the orders of one's superiors." We know that he was promoted to the rank of corporal. We also know that he was severely wounded and gassed, and that during the period of his convalescence he lost his sight. This temporary blindness may have been due to the gas or it may have been another manifestation of hysteria. It does not really matter. The important thing is that Hitler went through the war and through the revolution which put an end to the war and never at any moment seemed to have had the faintest suspicion of what it was all about. The big underlying forces that are at work among the German people and in every other part of the world completely escaped his attention. It was not that he was deliberately trying to ignore them. They just failed to exist for him, like music for a person who is tone-deaf. At best they annoyed him and disturbed him in his own dreams, and those dreams had little to do with the Brotherhood of Men and the Unity of Nations then so pathetically preached by those selfsame people who fifteen years later would either be dead or in a concentration camp, regretting the day when they had failed to realize that this absurd and bombastic fanatic had something which they themselves did not have, complete and unlimited faith in himself, and that he was so deeply convinced of the sacredness of his mission that he would stop at no crime to gain his point and would recognize no obligation toward ordinary principles of common decency if by breaking his word or his solemn promise he could advance his own interests.

It is true that he had already reached the point where he had begun to associate his own interests with those of Germany. This made it possible for him to persuade himself that whatever he did was done out of a feeling of profound patriotism. But that does not really make it any easier for his victims. They are just as dead as if he had never meant a word of what he said. And their exile will not be made any more bearable by the thought that they could have avoided all this if they had had the courage of their responsibilities and had treated this agitator who deliberately flaunted every law of the country that gave him hospitality as he today treats them in the country that gave him birth.

The war was over, and Hitler had lost the only real home he had ever known—a dugout which he had shared with a dozen comrades. His mother had long since died. His sisters had not heard of him for years and had not the vaguest idea what had become of him. Not a single woman cared whether he was dead or alive. Not having entirely recovered from his last attack of gas, he was sent to the country to recuperate. From there, for lack of anything better to do, he drifted back to Munich, which then was torn with bitter civil strife—open warfare between Red and White soldiers.

Hitler took the side of the Socialists against the Communists and apparently did considerable "intelligence work" for the regular army as soon as order had been re-established. "Intelligence service" is a polite expression for spying. Spying is not exactly an honorable profession. But it paid better than turning out "hand-painted" postal cards. These activities, however, occupied only part of his time. He had a lot of leisure and he could use his evenings as he pleased.

He gave up his amateur standing as a political agitator and turned professional. He was by no means a polished speaker, but he appealed to those Germans who liked their rhetoric raw, and God knows Hitler gave it to them without any frills. He could do this because he was a man with a natural sense of grievance and he was addressing himself to millions of his fellow men who had a twofold reason to feel themselves cheated by fate. In the first place, because they had lost a war which all along they had expected to win, and in the second place, because they had also been deprived of their jobs and saw no prospect of ever getting them back. It was then that Hitler began to realize that he had a most powerful ally. The name of this unexpected friend was Treaty of Versailles.

Peace treaties, ever since the beginning of written history, have as a rule been pretty bad. That is undoubtedly very regrettable, but to a certain degree it also seems unavoidable, for peace treaties are rarely concluded in an atmosphere of calm and serenity. Two or three years of mutual cruelties and wholesale slaughter have strained everybody's nerves to the breaking point, and the victor is in no mood to listen to the voice of reason. All his worst emotions have been thoroughly aroused. At last he has an opportunity to avenge the death of his friends. He must reimburse himself for the losses he has suffered. His enemy is at his mercy. Now let him suffer a few of the agonies he has forced upon others and above all things, let him pay!

The peace treaty of Versailles was no exception to this rule. Neither was it worse than most other peace treaties. It was just another peace treaty, and peace treaties, ever since the beginning of time, have, as a rule, been pretty bad.

The average German, who had spent four years fighting against terrific odds and who had been kept in complete ignorance about everything that had happened in the rest of the world, was hopelessly bewildered by those events which overnight seemed to have reduced his country from a powerful empire to the rank of a seventh-rate nation. Unable and unwilling to believe that all this was in any way his own fault, he looked for a scapegoat. Hitler was ready with a suitable candidate for this unpleasant honor. The Jew, the international Jew, who always grew fat upon the misfortunes of his Christian neighbors, that vile and perfidious monster, was at the bottom of Germany's downfall. Get rid of him and elect a strong leader who is 100% German so that that sort of thing could never happen again. He, the Austrian, was that 100% German for which all of them were looking. But they did not yet know it. So he undertook to tell them. He bought himself a raincoat which was to become the uniform of the army of liberation and started upon his new career.

We have neither the time nor the space to follow our budding dictator through the endless ups and downs that were so characteristic of the earlier days of all young politicians. Hitler had a very hard time of it because he could find no party that quite suited him. But in the end he joined a small group of war veterans who had organized themselves as the National Socialist German Workers' Party. The name was too long for most people. They abbreviated it into Nazi party. After a while it became just Nazi. It was an ugly flag to cover an even more repellent cargo.

The program of Hitler's new friends was not unlike that of most others. The country (it is hardly necessary to tell you this) had been betrayed by the capitalists and by the Jews. It was as simple as all that. The remedy was equally simple. Let prosperity be brought back to the masses of the people by getting rid of these two enemies of society.

For purely practical reasons, the hostility toward the capitalist classes was quickly dropped. It took money to run an election. The businessmen, although greatly impoverished, still had more money than anybody else. They also had more to lose than anybody else. Therefore they were willing to listen to reason, and as soon as they, too, began to suspect that a workingman's party on a non-Marxian basis might be of great help to them in their fight against Communism, they hastened to join forces with those they could no longer hope to defeat.

As for the Jews, they could not follow the example of their Christian neighbors, who also happened to be capitalists. They fitted too neatly into the campaign of hatred and suspicion which Hitler intended to start as soon as he was a little more certain of his own followers. Most contemporary observers seem to agree that the Jews, if given the opportunity, would also have accepted Hitler as their leader. But they were never given that chance. Hitler needed them for a different purpose of his own, as victims to be thrown to the mob, any time anything at home should go wrong and it was necessary to pacify the mob by a happy afternoon at the circus, throwing innocent people to the wild animals.

Oh, yes, I know the answer. "Dirty lies of the foreign press! Who ever saw a dead Jew lying on the corner of a German street?" But there are more refined ways of torture than by cutting a man's throat or breaking him on the wheel. And it is to that sort of torture I refer.

At first the National Socialist German Workers' Party made little headway. Nobody took it very seriously. What could one expect of an organization run by a crazy Austrian, who, even when he ordered himself a glass of beer in a public restaurant, talked as if he were addressing a mass meeting, and who during four years of war had never got any farther than being a mere corporal?

But Hitler's ego once more saved him. He knew all along that he would succeed, for was he not predestined for great things? He vowed to crush all those who should dare to oppose him in his ambitions. And he did. How? By being completely and absolutely himself. He addressed his words primarily to that part of the populace which had lost everything. He, the glorious failure, had never had anything. As a result, there was a complete understanding between the speaker and his audience. The audience felt instinctively that if they would only stick to him, they would go places, and they were right. They went places they had never even dreamed of going, such as London and Paris and Prague. And unless we are very careful, they may even decide to pay a visit to Washington.

The incredible folly of the Allies, who, even after the armistice, prolonged the blockade for another year, causing the death of thousands of children born during the years of starvation, made the Germans ready to listen to anyone who would cater to their sense of injustice and would appeal to their natural instincts of revenge. In Adolf Hitler they found a champion who told them everything they wanted to hear, for he throve on hatred as a baby thrives on milk.

Here we once more must pick up the analogy between the Führer and Robespierre.

At this particular moment in their careers, during the long and tedious years that separated them from their final success, both men fought a lonely battle and both came to the conclusion that the whole world was out of step with them. But neither of them had the slightest intention of getting into step with the rest of their fellow men. They would have regarded such a procedure as a sign of moral weakness, and moral weakness is the last thing of which we can accuse either of them. No, no, a thousand times no! Let the heavens fall and let hell spew forth its horrors, but they would follow the road they had mapped out for themselves. They could, of course, be killed. But they could not be made to deviate even a single inch from the path they had chosen.

To you and me, this would seem an untenable position. We are gregarious animals. We do our best to gain the good will of our fellow men and we simply will not set ourselves apart from our neighbors. Hitler and Robespierre never were under any obligation to set themselves apart. They were apart. Nature had seen to that. Their ego was a Chinese wall which kept them separated from the rest of humanity, and this arrangement suited them perfectly. Had they been normal human beings, they would sooner or later have surrendered from sheer loneliness. But they were never lonely. They always could withdraw inside their own shells. And once inside, they asked for no better company.

I must now give you a definition of two words which I shall have to use a great deal before I bid you farewell. They are not pleasant words, but neither is this a pleasant story.

The first one is the word "prig."

According to Noah Webster, a prig is "a person who offends or irritates by too obvious or rigid observation of the proprieties in speech, manners, conduct, or one self-sufficient in virtue," in short, a completely self-satisfied creature, who in his self-righteous blindness is convinced that no one approaches him in his perfection of character.

The other is the word "mucker."

According to the same source, a mucker is a "coarse,

vulgar person, especially one guilty of offense against standards of courtesy and honor."

In America we sometimes talk about a prig but we do not like to refer to one of our fellow men as a mucker. We seem to feel that it is a reflection upon a certain definite class of society and it goes against the traditions of our democracy to confess that there may be definite classes of society in a land where all men are supposed to have been born "equal." However, as I am talking about Europe, nobody need take offense and I can safely describe the success of both Robespierre and Hitler as the result of "a prig assuming the leadership over the mucker."

Of course, this comparison is not entirely fair, but that can't be helped. Economic conditions have changed so completely during the last century and a half that it is difficult to describe the Nazi revolution in terms of the French revolution. Robespierre addressed himself mainly to the proletariat—the neglected and submerged inhabitants of the evil-reeking slums of Paris, men and women who had nothing to lose and everything to gain because they had never owned anything at all except the rags on their backs and the children that sprawled over the floors of their dark and miserable tenements.

Hitler soon understood that that class of society could never be of any use to him. The German proletariat had already made its choice. It had chosen Lenin as its hero and it was rapidly moving in the direction of Moscow. The Germans who had made the revolution had no use for the ex-corporal. At best, they laughed at him. At worst, they threw brickbats.

Neither did the new Messiah at first have a much better chance with Big Business. For Big Business had expected that as soon as the war was over, everything would be as it always had been before. Big Business felt instinctively suspicious of a political program which made a point of denouncing with such particular bitterness all those who made profits by loaning out money at interest. They warmly sympathized with a leader who was so bitter in his hatred of the wicked Bolsheviks that he wanted to see them all strung up from the nearest lampposts and who foamed at the mouth every time he had to refer to the name of the international Jew, Karl Marx. Because Hitler pretended to be the sworn enemy of all Socialists and Communists, Big Business would occasionally slip an unobtrusive amount of money (cash preferred to checks) into the hands of this maniac with the anti-Jewish obsessions, but it was very careful not to take sides. At least, not until it would know a little more definitely which way the fellow meant to go, and whether, after all, he too was not some sort of disguised Communist.

There remained the remnants of the old army, reduced to very small proportions both by violent death upon the field of battle and by the stipulations of the Treaty of Versailles, which had changed the soldiers of the Kaiser into a sort of superpolicemen, just powerful enough to keep the Bolshevik elements of the Republic in their proper place. But these professional military gentlemen stuck closely to their old code of behavior. According to that code, the colonel did not associate with the corporal. This one particular corporal was undoubtedly talking sense when he told the

German people that their armies had never been defeated on the field of battle and that the collapse of the Empire had been due to the machinations of the internationally minded Jews, who had broken up the morale behind the front. But just the same, he was a former corporal and there were certain things a gentleman did not do. Why, the fellow was not even *satisfaktionsfähig*. He belonged to a class of society with whom one could never expect to settle an affair of honor by an appeal to the saber or the pistol. So, no matter how eloquently he might rave about a rejuvenated Germany, ready to lick the whole world and make Central Europe safe for the people of pure Teutonic blood, he was still too much the corporal to let one take the risk of being seen in his company. Later, perhaps, but most certainly not now. Germany was full of all sorts of noisy self-appointed prophets, crazy fellows with crazy ideas and forever asking for everybody's support. For the time being, it was enough to drill the few remaining soldiers of the regular army so that each one of them might be able to qualify as an officer, if the Day of Vengeance should ever come. Meanwhile, the corporal was a safe bet, for no matter how you treated him, he would always snap to attention the moment he came face to face with one of his superiors.

As a result, there remained only one group of people to whom Hitler could address himself with a reasonable expectation that he would find them sympathetic to his ideas, and these were the small shopkeepers, the small tradesmen, the whole of what Europe

calls the *petite bourgeoisie*, people who were separated from the out-and-out proletariat by the tenacity
with which they will stick to a semblance of respectability long after they have lost everything else.

During the Great War that class of society had
given more than its quota of soldiers to their Imperial
Master, and hundreds of thousands of them had been
slaughtered to further the career of some obtuse general who never, in private life, would have conde-
scended to speak to the parents of his obedient cannon fodder. When things had begun to go wrong, this
class had surrendered the last pfennigs of its painfully
saved little nest eggs to the government and in return
had received beautifully engraved pieces of paper that
were now completely worthless. It had provided
against old age and a possible rainy day by taking out
annuities and life insurance, and these policies had
now lost all value. It had, according to the best of its
abilities, built homes in which to bring up its children
and give them a better chance in life than the parents
themselves had ever enjoyed.

Now everything—absolutely everything—was gone.
The cruel stipulations of the Versailles Treaty had
loaded the German people with a debt which it never
could hope to pay. That lower middle class, therefore,
cut loose from its ancient moorings, was drifting aim-
lessly upon the turbulent waves of the great sea of unrest and revolution that followed in the wake of the
war. It clamored loudly for someone who would once
more take hold of its rudderless craft and who would
conduct it to some safe port, any port at all, no matter
how humble but assuring the crew that which it

craved most of all—security and safety and just a little hope for the day of tomorrow.

To these poor shipwrecked mariners, scandalously betrayed by their former masters, Adolf Hitler and his ambitious plans were no joke. On the contrary, he was the long-expected Messiah. And if, in order to follow him, his disciples must swallow a great many ideas that hardly appealed to them, very well, they would do the swallowing, for anything was better than the present unbearable state of anarchy with French Negroes let loose upon the defenseless people of the Rhineland and half-clad Moscovites threatening the frontier on the other side of the country.

Yes, good reader, laugh at Hitler, hate him and despise him, but remember that we ourselves put him where he is, we, the proud democracies of the West, who tortured a vanquished enemy until, having lost all hope, the victims of our vengeance and indifference were ready for any act of desperation and willing to entrust their fate to an obscure ex-corporal of the old imperial army, who had very little to recommend himself except that he endlessly preached the one gospel to which every German was most eager to listen, a gospel of hate and revenge, based upon the command- ment, "Thou shalt get even."

We in America, having spent most of our days liv- ing peacefully with our German neighbors whom we have always respected for their sound qualities of hon- esty and decency, their good-natured humor, their love for their homes and their devotion to their wives and children, we find it difficult to understand what happened in the old country during the years immediately after the Great War. And we ask, "Where does the mucker come in, that detestable creature you described a moment ago?" I will tell you. He came in when Hitler was beginning to look for recruits willing to do any sort of dirty work, so that at last he could beat down the resistance of his enemies and make a bid for the government.

And who was this mucker, socially and economically speaking?

He was the son of respectable parents, who in happier days had belonged to the lower middle class. He was too young to have seen any actual service, but he had spent the impressionable years of his life in an atmosphere of violence and starvation. If he happened to have been the son of a farmer, he would not have fared quite so badly, for in the country he could always have found something to eat. The soil is kind to those who are its friends, but, unfortunately, one cannot raise potatoes on the pavements of Essen or Berlin any more than one can hope to grow corn on the asphalt of upper Broadway or Times Square.

But the mucker was rarely the son of a farmer. As a rule, he was one of the brood of some little shopkeeper or tradesman, who in happier days had catered to the needs of the industrial workers of this highly industrialized nation. These industrial workers were now unemployed. The dole they received was not of American proportions. It kept the recipients alive but little more than that. And the shopkeeper, no matter how well disposed, could not extend credit for more than a few months. After that, he too was forced to close up shop and to accept charity.

Having been raised according to a very strict code of conduct, he himself stuck faithfully to a few of his old rules of behavior, for such habits, acquired during many generations by people "who knew their place" are very tenacious and they will stick long after everything else is gone. But the younger generation had not enjoyed the inestimable privileges of such a sound bringing-up while they were children. Father had been away at the front. Mother had slaved day and night to find scraps of food for her offspring and to keep a roof over their heads. As a result, the kids had been left to shift for themselves.

Now they were nineteen years of age or twenty or twenty-one and they were underfed, calloused by the hideous things they had seen as children, and worst of all, they were without any prospects for the future. It was unavoidable that they should feel themselves cheated out of their birthright. They could never expect to succeed their fathers in the old shop that had belonged to their families for so many years, because the shop was gone. They could not even expect to learn a trade, for the factories were closed. To change their white collars for a pair of overalls meant of course a step downward on the social ladder, but it would have been much better than nothing at all. But the few plants that still had orders were working for the benefit of a foreign nation or had been turned into barracks for regiments of savages from northern Africa and labor battalions from Asia. Never before in history had an entire group of young people faced a future so completely devoid of hope.

It was these disinherited sons of the respectable middle classes that had been ruined by both war and peace which provided Hitler with that mucker element which he needed if he ever were to wrest the power away from the men who were then ruling the German Republic and make himself the dictator of a new and united Reich. Revolutions are a messy business at best and one cannot be too squeamish in the choice of one's assistants while trying to replace one form of society by another. And whatever their faults, these neglected children of the slums were most certainly not squeamish. They had been brought up in the belief that violence was the only way in which a man could get what he wanted. Had not that glorious war been an officially sanctioned expression of the idea of "might over right?" And these boys and girls were products of that war. They had never seen or heard anything but fighting during their most impressionable years. The only appeals that had ever been made to their emotions were appeals for greater efforts along the lines of brutality and ferocity. The nobler aspirations of mankind had never touched them. The gentler arts of peace were unknown to them. And even if they had heard of them, they now regarded them only in a spirit of profound contempt. One did not paint pictures in the trenches and one did not start a sonnet while getting ready for a charge across No Man's Land. They knew, because their fathers had told them so when they were home on a few days' leave. Nor could one hope to obtain a mitigation of the draconian laws which the French had forced upon the citizens of the Ruhr by telling Monsieur Poincaré about the perfections of Goethe's prose. A frosty stare would be all one would have got for one's trouble. So why bother about all this cumbersome cultural ballast when a well-stocked arsenal was a much more valuable national asset than a museum filled with masterpieces gathered together from every corner of the world?

The mucker is not a pleasant person to deal with. We have reason to know for we have a few of them right here in our own fair land. But like the rest of us, he is the product of his original surroundings. In the case of Germany, we ourselves provided those surroundings. Now we are being punished for our lack of foresight, and if we know our business, we shall prepare for the day when we must slay the creature or run the risk of being destroyed by him. By him and his rapidly increasing and hideous offspring.

Adolf Hitler despised Woodrow Wilson but he followed his example in starting his campaign on the basis of a definite number of points. Most of these famous 25 Points which constituted the political program of the new Nazi party have remained a dead letter. By the way, they were not of Hitler's own hand. He had little gift for that sort of constructive labor and the 25 Points were the work of one of his earliest partners, a Bavarian engineer by the name of Gottfried Feder. This man Feder was a half-baked inventor, who, in the years before the war, had tried to construct ships out of cement and who during the war itself had favored the government with a memorandum suggesting that Germany get rid of its rapidly increasing debt, by the simple (if not exactly honest) expedient of going bankrupt. At one time in his career, Feder had also been a serious student of the doctrines of Karl Marx, but he had come to somewhat different conclusions from his teacher. For example he had discovered that capital in the hands of a Christian would be of benefit to the community, whereas the same capital when owned by a Jew would invariably corrupt the state and lead to disaster. This slightly muddleheaded financial genius now provided the new party with a political and economic program of its own. Let me recite a few of the 25 Points upon the basis of which the Nazis asked for the support of the German electorate.

Germany must of course belong to the Germans (the word Aryan had not yet made its appearance) and all people of "foreign blood" (read: "all Jews") must be expelled. The Treaty of Versailles had to be scrapped. Germany had to rearm and become more powerful than ever before. No one was to enjoy the benefits of an "unearned income," whatever that might mean. The rate of interest had to be greatly diminished unless it should prove possible to abolish interest altogether. All department stores must be surrendered to German owners and must become the property of the state. And so on. And so forth.

It sounds rather absurd, this program, but every article and paragraph was a cleverly worded invitation to the members of the lower middle class to join this new organization which promised to lead them out of the house of bondage (Jewish bondage) and would bring about a return of the old prewar prosperity and respectability.

As for the mucker, who understood little about the intricacies of political theory and cared less, he too found among these 25 Points a great many things that appealed to him. Germany's downfall, so they were told for the hundred thousandth time, was not the result of an unsuccessful war, waged by incompetent generals, but it had been brought about by the "enemy in the rear." That enemy in the rear was the Jew. Therefore let us go out in the street and beat up the first Jewish swine we meet. He may be the same man whose generosity had kept us from starving to death, in the years immediately after the war. But his soup kitchen was of course financed by the money he had stolen out of our own pockets. So to hell with gratitude and kill the Jew and take everything he has, for it really belongs to us who never did a stroke of work in our lives!

Those who think that I exaggerate are respectfully referred to the literature that exists upon the subject. Therein they will find many of the delightful songs that gained such enormous and deserved popularity during the days our friend Adolf was changing his ragged mob of ill-trained retainers into regiments of highly disciplined Storm Troopers and Schutzstaffeln, all of them provided with new brown shirts, beautiful high boots (making them feel as if they were real soldiers) and with very effective bludgeons and cudgels to be used at the pleasure of their owners for the purpose of convincing possible opponents of the errors of their views. A hundred years from now, when Hitler will be only an evil memory, these battle hymns may make interesting reading. Today they only fill us with a feeling of despair about humanity in general. Here was the most enlightened and best-educated nation in the world, and it used the same language that had given us *Ueber allen Gipfeln ist Ruh* to write the *Horst Wessel Lied*.

All of us are apt to be very dense at times. Some ten years ago, revisiting the happiest scenes of my youth in the lovely old city of Munich, I was taken by a friend (since then murdered by Adolf's henchmen) to a restaurant in the Theatiner Strasse and we walked past the Feldherrnhalle.

"Here is where the Nazis were shot down," the good, nearsighted Fritz remarked, and I, being a little hazy about that historic incident, asked, "When?"

"In November of 1923," he answered, "during the Beer Hall Putsch."

Then of course I remembered. Hitler, who repeatedly had promised the Bavarian authorities on his word of honor, that he would not try to upset the existing form of government by violence and that he would use only constitutional methods to achieve his ends, had tried to start a revolution at a meeting in the Hofbräuhaus. This attempt had failed and thereupon the following morning he had tried to make the Munich people rally to his colors by marching boldly through the streets of their city at the head of his private army of his henchmen. He had assured himself of the support of General Ludendorff, the man who had won the war for the Allies. The General, living in supposed retirement near Munich, was now seeing spooks and was dabbling in strange religious beliefs, even dreaming of a return of old Wotan and Thor. But among the rank and file of the Germans he was still a popular idol, and Hitler was certain that no German soldier would ever dare to lift his rifle against his former chief-of-staff.

But in this he was mistaken. The soldiers of the regular army apparently had more respect for their given word than the leader of the Nazi party. When the Nazis disobeyed the command to stop, they fired a volley and the result had been terrible. Fourteen Nazis lay dead on the pavement of that open space, where in happier days we used to listen to the music of the Guards' band. The others, overcome by panic, had fled, except old Ludendorff, who all alone had quietly marched on as if no bullet could touch him, and had thereupon been made a prisoner by the troops of the Republic.

As for Hitler, he had obeyed a perfectly normal instinct and, flat on his tummy, he had waited until the firing ceased. Whether, as his admirers assure us, he had been pulled down by a friend who had been mortally wounded or, as his enemies claim, he had let himself fall on his face without outside assistance, that we do not know and it really makes no difference. Only a fool would have stood up under such a fusillade and, unfortunately for the rest of us, on that day of all days, Hitler behaved like a completely normal human being and, regardless of his pride and his mission, had preferred safety to death.

Nor can we blame him that, once the battle had been lost, he did his best to escape. In falling down (or in being pulled down) he had dislocated his shoulder blade and he needed prompt medical attention. His friends rushed him into a car which they had found somewhere and drove him to the Starnberg Lake where Putzi Hanfstaengl's mother and sister fixed his arm and took care of him until he was arrested by the Bavarian authorities.

He had deliberately broken his word and, regardless of his solemn promises, he had tried to overthrow the existing form of government by force and violence. In addition to this, he was now responsible for the death of sixteen of his followers (two more had died of their wounds and one more was to die a few days later) and for all this he was condemned to five years of very mild detention in a fortress. After nine months of residence in a modern prison, provided with more comforts than he had ever enjoyed in all his life, he was released. But those nine months had given him a most welcome rest and furthermore had provided him with the opportunity to write his famous volume of memoirs and political prognostications known as *My Battle*.

His friend Rudolph Hess had helped him with his labors and when the book was published, the Nazi party had not only its own prophet but also its own Bible. The latest edition of 1938 (which I have as well as the first) states that up to date not less than 3,980,000 copies of this book have been sold in Germany alone. Hitler may have been a very poor author, but only in one sense of the word, for his book made both him and his publisher rich.

Let me say however that I put absolutely no credence in those stories which love to dwell upon the treasures which Hitler is supposed to have gathered from his book and from other sources and which are said to have been deposited in a number of foreign banks for a possible rainy day. The man does not think in terms of private gain. What would he do with money? He needed a lot of ready cash during the time he was struggling for power but afterwards it meant nothing to him. For he had the one thing in the world he cared for. He had power.

His final rise to fame and glory is too well known to need repeating. The weak and vacillating government of the Republic did not have the courage to suppress this most dangerous and unscrupulous enemy, and Hitler's Storm Troopers, now certain of immunity from punishment for whatever damage they might inflict upon their opponents, established a widespread reign of terror. They were so effective with their bludgeons that most people were afraid to go to the polls and that is exactly what they had hoped to accomplish.

But even then the rise in the number of Nazi representatives in the German parliament was very slow and in November of the year 1932 it looked as if there were to be a complete deadlock. Old Field Marshal von Hindenburg, the one outstanding military figure among the Germans who had remained faithful to his soldiers even after their defeat, had been elected president because his prestige was such that no one dared to oppose him. But he was in his eighties. He was beginning to forget things. He forgot even the intense dislike he had felt for the clumsy "Bohemian corporal," as he had called Adolf Hitler after he had met him for the first time. And now all sorts of crafty political sceneshifters, realizing that soon some sort of a permanent decision would have to be made, set to work to forward the interests of their own particular candidates. Regardless of the interests of the country.

Meanwhile the majority of the German people had grown deadly tired of this everlasting wrangling, this never-ceasing unrest. There still was a parliament but it talked and debated and did nothing at all about the rapidly increasing number of unemployed. The inflation had destroyed what the greed of the Allies and domestic revolutions had left. The malicious Franz von Papen, of painful and incendiary memory in our own country and by and large the most objectionable and despicable figure in the history of Germany during the last twenty years, was as usual stirring up trouble in the muddy political waters that threatened to engulf even the presidential residence. And Big Business (combined with the powerful country squires from East Prussia) decided that the time had come at last to take this little man with the big voice seriously. They prevailed upon President von Hindenburg to appoint a cabinet of the Right and to make Hitler his Chancellor, while at the same time calling in a few of their conservative friends so as to act as a balance wheel in case the Corporal should go on the warpath.

It is quite right, therefore, to say that Hitler was not elected to office by a majority of the votes of his fellow Germans but was smuggled into the governmental palace through the kitchen entrance to help the gentlemen on the ground floor protect themselves against the liberal and radical elements in the country. But what does it matter at this late date how and in what manner the Führer came to power? He is the head of the strongest, the most brutal and the most ruthless military dictatorship in our modern world. And that is all we should remember just now.

The leaders of the democratic nations who at that moment could still have prevented a development which now threatens their own safety apparently lacked the necessary imagination to foresee what would happen if they let Hitler have his way. In consequence whereof they can no longer be counted among the first-class nations of the world, and unless we are very careful we shall go the same way as France and the British Empire.

Democracy is the most unnatural, the most artificial, and therefore the most difficult of all forms of government. Unless it enjoys the constant and most devoted care of all its adherents all of the time, it will invariably come to grief through lack of co-operation and self-discipline. Since Democracy is essentially a state of mind—a philosophy of life—a way of feeling —it is not something you can learn out of a book.

The Germans, who have no gift to learn from life but depend entirely upon book learning, had never known how to handle Democracy. In 1848 they had made a pathetic failure of their attempt to rule themselves. And now between the years 1918 and 1933 they repeated all the mistakes they had made in 1848. In 1848, the final result had been one Otto von Bismarck. In 1933, the final result was one Adolf Hitler.

I would give a great deal if by means of some ingenious television apparatus I could watch the face of old Bismarck as he studies the present occupant of that chair which he himself graced half a century ago. I can even hear him grumble, "The *Böhmischer Gefreiter* had an easy time of it at Berchtesgaden and at Munich. I had to deal with a very different sort of opponent. I wish that little Adolf had been obliged to run up against him! He then would have been taught a lesson he would never have been able to forget. But Disraeli was a Jew. Lucky for Hitler that Chamberlain was not!"

On the night of February 27th of the year 1933 the building of the Reichstag in Berlin caught fire and was almost completely destroyed. Except for a few of Herr Hitler's most rabid followers, I doubt whether there are many people who today are in any doubt about this beautifully timed piece of arson. The whole thing had been most carefully organized by the Nazis themselves. Even the Supreme Court of Germany, called upon to try the supposed culprits, was obliged to confess that most of them were innocent. An exception was made in the case of a Dutch boy, a degenerate and half-wit, who, by an appeal to his vanity, had been prevailed upon to play the stellar role in this tragedy and who paid for his hour of short-lived glory by having his head chopped off.

The others were reluctantly set free. But for the moment at least, the desired effect had been reached. The wise Communists and Socialists and their colleagues of the Catholic party correctly interpreted the red glow against the Berlin sky that spelled their doom and fled for their lives. Those who remained in Germany kept away from the polls. During the panic that followed upon this latest "Outrage of the Communist, who would not even stop short at arson" (as the Nazi papers shrieked with trumped-up fury), Hitler was able to rid himself of all his more dangerous enemies. An obedient parliament (or what remained of it, now that all the old leaders were gone) bestowed dictatorial powers upon the new leader. And after the death of Marshal von Hindenburg, who did not survive this excitement very long, Hitler decreed that there never would be another President of Germany. There would be a Führer—a leader of the realm (a "big boss," as the boys of Tammany Hall would call him). For the rest of his natural life, Hitler himself would be that Führer.

France and England did not like this. They began to have vague suspicions about what might happen if this man ran away with things. But they refrained from interfering. Germany had now been set free from the menace of Bolshevism and could therefore be counted on to be on their side in their war upon Communism. For the moment that was all that mattered.

That this latest development would eventually lead to the disastrous Second Treaty of Versailles—the infamous agreement of Munich of September of the year 1938—that of course was something they could not possibly foretell. Even had they suspected anything of the sort, I doubt whether they would have acted differently. For the moment at least, Moscow had been checkmated and all was well with the world.

Once Hitler reigned supreme, the dance of death of Democracy began in all seriousness. It would take the brush of a Holbein to do justice to this picture and to show us what happened when the democracies of the West had proved themselves too selfish or too blind or too weak to stand up for their rights while it was still possible to save the world from the terrible consequences of this new gospel of hate.

Within Germany itself, as the Nazi enthusiasts never tire of telling us, such tremendous strides forward have been made that one would never recognize the country if one knew it only from the days of the Republic.

The number of unemployed was reduced by eighty per cent, which is probably correct. But part of these are now engaged in the gigantic rearmament business and are therefore not doing any really useful work. The younger members of society are kept busy in the different labor camps. Hundreds of thousands of others have been pushed into the jobs left vacant by the Jews, who were deprived of their possessions and who were reduced to the rank of pariahs, a race of wanderers without a country, without the right to own property, without any ordinary civil rights, and therefore completely at the mercy of anything their executioners might feel inclined to do to them.

It cannot be denied that the production of raw materials has been increased enormously. But most of that increase too, has gone toward rearmament. Fast automobile roads have been built from one end of the country to the other, but these too serve primarily a military purpose. And due to the brilliant financial juggling of Dr. Hjalmar Schacht (a product of our Brooklyn public schools), Germany, as it proudly boasts, has been able to accomplish all this without any foreign assistance.

But what are the actual results when examined without the stimulating help of one of Dr. Goebbels' brass bands and removed from the threat of a concentration camp? The armament expenditures today are four times as great as they were when the Nazis came to power. Foreign credits have been cut off on all sides. The production of food has remained the same as in 1932 and the German laboring man of today gets fewer of the essentials of life than he did four years ago when Hitler came to power. I know that he is now supposed to have a job but there must still be a great many who are less lucky, for the wage earners are obliged to surrender more than twenty per cent of their income to pay for the relief of their less fortunate brethren.

And the German worker has been most completely deprived of his former freedom. He is in the same position as his colleagues across the Alps. He is not allowed to organize. Neither can he go on strike. To compensate him for his lack of liberty, he now enjoys a two weeks' holiday with pay, and at very reasonable rates he can see all the best plays and hear all the best music, provided that they were neither written nor composed by a non-Aryan, which, especially within the realm of literature and music, leaves him very little choice. The farmer, being assured of his farm, also enjoys a degree of security which he had not had for years. But he too is no longer a free agent. He is almost as much "bound to the earth" as a medieval serf.

All this may sound incredible to our honest American ears. "Why don't these people do something about this?" we feel inclined to ask. "Why do they accept the rule of this little man who has more power over them than a Russian landowner of the eighteenth century had over his serfs?" Because—and have no doubt about it!—that little man with the eyes of a sleepwalker has been able to perform the one miracle for which all Germans were waiting, even those who had every reason to hate him.

He has given his adopted fellow countrymen a new religion, a new Illusion; he has given them a renewed faith in the destiny of their own race. He came to them at a moment when, defeated in war and impoverished by peace, they had lost all hope. By his endless harping upon the same subject, his strident voice was at last able to convince them that they had not really lost the war, but had been betrayed by their Jewish and Communist enemies at home. And so, at last, they once more have something to live for and, if need comes, to die for—a new belief in themselves, a new pride in their past achievements, a fresh faith in their own glorious future.

With all this, none of us can possibly find fault. On the contrary, we should rejoice when a friendly fellow nation overcomes its difficulties and is once more willing to assume its share of the burdens of our common civilization. But when such a creed arrogantly proclaims that it has a monopoly upon all virtues and violently denies the good right of others to seek salvation after their own particular fashion, then it is time to call a halt. And that is the point we have reached at this particular moment. Hence these words of warning.

I am looking at the map of the world and this is what I see:

A France so pathetically weakened by internal strife that it is unable to act.

A Russia so hopelessly weakened by internal strife that it is unable to assert itself and can only talk and denounce those who tell us the truth about its far-famed military preparations.

A British Empire which seems to have reached a point (so common in the history of all empires) at which it has grown too old and too tired to be willing to assume any further responsibilities for the safety of either its own dominions or the world at large.

A Japanese nation which has surrendered to a small military clique and has now gone on a rampage, running amok like some poor, drug-soaked coolie, stabbing away indiscriminately at any living being that it encounters along the road that is supposed to lead to glory.

A powerful Italian dictatorship, so bewildered and upset by the results of its recent alliance with Germany, that it does not quite know what to do or where to go, nor what choice to make next.

A Spain, torn to pieces horribly by internal strife and sacrificing the best of its sons for the ultimate benefit of its greedy and covetous neighbors.

A mere handful of small European nations, still decently governed and bravely trying to maintain themselves and to remain faithful to their old ideals of freedom and independence against the aggressions of an irresponsible visionary who regards the whole of Europe as so much Teutonic hinterland, to be occupied by his armies according to his pleasure.

The memory of that fair Austrian land which now lies helpless before the fury of a man who can never forget that it rejected him and made him feel his own insignificance.

A Czechoslovakian Republic which, with all its faults (very minor ones at that) remained the last bulwark of democracy in Central Europe, but was betrayed by its allies and sacrificed upon the altar of necessity by those who did not seem to realize that in signing the death warrant of Prague, they also signed the death warrants of London and Paris.

A score of other Central European powers, falling upon the lacerated body of their Czechoslovakian neighbor with the hungry ferocity of wolves who are attacking a deer that has been mortally wounded and has been left to its own devices by the other members of the herd.

A score of South American republics, struggling in the coils of a most perfidious but clever sort of propaganda, which is gradually laming them and is preparing them for that death thrust which they no longer know how to avert.

And everywhere, panic—sheer, blind panic—which has killed all reason, which has stifled all nobler feelings, which makes its victims ready to strike at anything and everything, like the beasts in the jungle overtaken by a forest fire.

Only one nation—only one people—still stand free and independent and able to act as the champion of human rights.

That nation is the much hated Democracy of the West.

That nation is the United States of America.

I know the answer. Mr. Hoover and our ambassador to the Court of St. James have just stated it. Why all this show of impassioned rhetoric? Why urge us to take part in a quarrel that is really no business of ours? We have the Atlantic, the blessed Atlantic, which separates us from the Old World by three thousand miles of open sea. Surely, we do not expect the German airplanes to come and drop bombs on New York and Philadelphia? Even that theory about German airplane carriers, penetrating into the Hudson Bay, is a little farfetched, for our navy could easily take care of them. Europe has never meant anything to us except a profound and prolonged headache. Why bother?

If we don't go over there, Hitler surely won't come over here!

Are you quite sure of that? Have you any certainty that he won't find some pretext to come over here and do unto us what he has done to the European democracies? I grant you that we are not in such immediate danger as, for example, Denmark or Holland or Switzerland. From a military point of view, we are still safe enough. But I am not thinking of airplanes and submarines nor of the battalions that will follow in their wake. I am thinking of another weapon, quite as powerful and in some ways even more efficient than mere brute force. I am thinking of that form of propaganda which, like some deadly gas, does its work so quietly yet so efficiently that the victim does not even suspect its existence until his will has been completely paralyzed and he is no longer able to offer any sort of resistance.

That particular sort of poisonous gas of propaganda is of very recent origin. It has allowed Adolf Hitler to defeat his enemies and to conquer Central Europe without the firing of a single shot.

Adolf Hitler has many henchmen. Those who might have threatened his own safety by reminding him of some of the promises of social improvement he had made during his bid for power—they no longer need worry him. They are dead. The mass murders of the 30th of June of the year 1934, when the Führer, as the final arbiter of the fate of Germany, ordered the extermination of over a thousand of his former friends and associates—that holocaust, known as the Great Purge, has set him free from the threat of mutiny within the ranks of his own followers. Should occasion arise, he will undoubtedly act again with the same savagery as in 1934, and so he is at liberty to march forward, regardless of what might happen at home.

At the same time he cannot possibly attend to every detail of government by himself. He must rely upon the services of a few trusted retainers. They are a motley crew and a most unsavory group, according to our way of thinking. They are not even Germans, for most of them were born abroad in Africa or South America or Russia. But all of them are now 100 per cent Nazis and they rule supreme over the land of their adoption, like the gangsters from half a dozen countries who until recently were in control of a great many of our big cities. And with the exception of Alfred Rosenberg, a native of Esthonia and the philosopher (God save the mark!) of the Nazi movement, they play only minor roles in the government of the Third Reich and therefore need not worry us as much as two other men who are native Germans and form part of the all-highest Nazi triumvirate.

They are Hermann Goering and Dr. Paul Joseph Goebbels. Of these two, we can also dismiss Goering as being much of a threat to our national existence. He is the reincarnation of the medieval German *Landsknecht*, the boisterous, vainglorious professional rowdy, who loved a fight for the sake of the fight and the fun of rolling in the mud with an adversary. The type is familiar to us from a large number of books and plays that have been written upon the subject.

But the *Landsknecht*, like his Italian equivalent, the *condottiere*, is now merely an historical curiosity and no longer a menace. In the case of Hermann Goering, he would adore chasing all over Europe at the head of his squadrons of airplanes, just as Murat (whom he resembles in a great many ways) loved nothing more dearly than to lead Napoleon's cavalry against any sort of an enemy, from a handful of Polish peasants to a regiment of Russian Dragoons. Being a sick man (due to wounds honorably acquired during the Great War) and most intemperate in the expression of his emotions, Goering will probably die a sudden death, fulminating in his own particular brand of billingsgate against those whom he hates most of all—those opponents who can still lay claim to the word "gentleman."

Far different is the case of Dr. Paul Joseph Goebbels. When I hear his name, I unconsciously think back to that lovely evening in Salzburg when I watched a performance of Reinhardt's *Everyman*. It seemed that that marvelous showman had concentrated all his efforts upon his Devil. Even now, after almost six years, that Devil gives me the creeps. He was everything a perfect Devil should be. So is Dr. Paul Joseph Goebbels.

Physical infirmity can do one of two things to a man. It can either soften his temperament and change him into a kindly and understanding citizen, whose own misfortunes have made him all the more ready to take pity upon the foibles and shortcomings of his neighbors. Or it can embitter him to the point where he becomes a fiend, forever trying to get even with a world that has not been fair to him, and deriving a malicious joy from inflicting pain upon those who have not been cursed the way he has been.

Paul Joseph Goebbels belongs to the latter class, and by and large I would like to call him the most unattractive, because he is the least honest of the men who surround the Führer. Also, perhaps, the most dangerous because he is so well suited for the job entrusted to him—the job of poisoning the world with Hitler propaganda. To the Führer, that man alone is worth a thousand regiments, for it is Goebbels who has made it possible for Adolf Hitler to win his battles without the sacrifice of a single man or the firing of a single shot.

Goebbels has no gift for leadership. And most of the Nazis despise him just as the followers of Napoleon despised Talleyrand, his unscrupulous Minister of Foreign Affairs, who was the complete counterpart of "the Doctor," as Goebbels is commonly known. Except that Talleyrand betrayed every sovereign for whom he ever worked, while Goebbels feels a blind devotion toward the master who has made him what he is today—the head of the German propaganda service.

Curiously enough, the Doctor is the only one among the Nazi chiefs whose racial antecedents are not entirely above suspicion. He looks slightly Jewish but that, as all students of this subject know, means nothing at all. His fellow students in the days he studied the history of literature (with a Jewish professor) used to refer to him as "the Rabbi," but that also is without any particular significance. Only a careful study among his immediate ancestors could show us the truth and such an investigation is out of the question.

There is one item, however, which makes it very likely that this son of pious Catholic parents is really a descendant of some obscure Spanish-Jewish refugee who in the sixteenth century had found his way to the Rhineland. I refer to the man's implacable hatred for everything Jewish. There are no more relentless enemies of the Jewish race than those who are conscious of having Jewish blood in their own veins. The worst and the most cruel of all Spanish inquisitors was undoubtedly of Jewish origin. If I had time to look them up, I could enumerate quite a number of others. But the fact is well known to all of us who have ever listened to the bitter denunciations of the Jewish race by some one whose own grandfather or great-grandfather had belonged to the Synagogue. Personally therefore, I would rate him as a "doubtful case" like Richard Wagner.

From what I have written in some of my previous chapters, you might have come to the conclusion that Robespierre was my candidate for the incarnation of all that is most despicable in the human race. But Robespierre had one saving grace which put him slightly ahead of the eminent Dr. Goebbels. Robespierre at least believed in everything he said. Goebbels believes in nothing he says. Robespierre was animated by an ideal of virtue and righteousness—a misguided ideal, but an ideal just the same. Goebbels acts under no such delusion. He loves evil for evil's sake. It is his way of getting even with his fate. And therefore, long after all his other supporters shall have left him, Adolf Hitler can still count upon his friend, the Doctor—which, after all, is quite natural. The two men share the same religion—the religion of hate.

By now the world at large knows pretty well what Hitler wants and what he expects to do during the next half dozen years. He is no devotee of that old-fashioned sort of "secret diplomacy," which was supposed to have come to an end in the year 1918. He belongs more to the school of Bismarck, although Bismarck, with the traditions of his class, observed certain outward semblances of good manners and courtesy even when he had his enemy at his mercy and therefore, according to the Hitler code of ethics, was at perfect liberty to kick him in the face and call him names which are rarely heard outside of a sailors' dive on the waterfront of Hamburg or Bremen. For convenience' sake I have drawn up a brief list of Adolf Hitler's plans for the near future. Events are moving so fast that it is almost impossible to keep up with the latest developments, but I have tried to be as accurate as possible and here is the list.

1. When Hitler came to power, he wanted to rearm and make Germany the most powerful nation in the world. That has been done.
2. He wanted to make Austria a part of his Greater Germany. That has been done.
3. He wanted to militarize the Rhineland. Has been done.
4. He wanted to get hold of the Saar. Has been done.
5. He wanted to fortify his western border and make it as strong as France's famous Maginot Line. Has been done.

6. He wanted to get hold of Danzig. The Nazis today are in full control of Danzig, even if outwardly the city is not yet part of the Third Reich.

7. He wanted to get hold of Memel. He can take the city any time he likes.

8. He wanted to abolish the Polish Corridor. This he has not yet accomplished, but it will come very soon, as soon as he no longer needs Poland in his war upon Czechoslovakia.

9. He wanted to destroy Czechoslovakia as a democratic menace to his own eastern front. He has done this and, thanks to Messrs. Chamberlain and Daladier, in a most successful way.

10. He wanted to assist Franco in Spain so that afterwards, Spain's natural riches would be at Germany's disposal. He is still working at that.

11. He wanted to regain the German colonies in Africa and in the Pacific Ocean. He is now discussing this matter with France and England who, after their defeat in Munich, have no other choice but to give him what he wants and who at any moment may ask Portugal to follow Czechoslovakia's example and sacrifice part of its own territory to preserve the peace of Europe.

12. He wanted to frighten England in the Far East so as to make the British Empire more conciliatory in dealing with him in the West. The Japanese-German alliance was concluded for that express purpose and, as a result, England may have to withdraw from Hong Kong and her other Chinese possessions and retreat to Singapore.

13. He wanted to conclude an alliance with a European power that would strengthen his position in dealing with France and England. The Berlin-Rome axis is there to show how successful he has been.

14. He wanted to imperil England's position in the Near East and weaken her prestige among the Moslems.

The daily news reports from Palestine are telling us of his almost complete success.

15. He wanted to regain the Danish-speaking territory in northern Germany, which the Allies had given to Denmark. He can take it whenever he wants it. The Danes won't fight. They will give it back to him with their blessing.

16. He wanted (pardon me for bringing this up) to set the Germans in the Tyrol free from Italian domination. For the moment, however, this matter seems to have become less urgent but one can always keep it on ice.

17. He wanted to start trouble in Ireland by suggesting to Mr. De Valera that he insist upon "self-determination" for the Catholic inhabitants of Ulster. Mr. De Valera lent a most willing ear, and in this way he is now most generously contributing to the difficulties of Downing Street.

18. He wanted to give Washington something to worry about by an intensive pro-Nazi propaganda in Mexico and in every South American and Central American republic. He would have been completely successful if Washington had been less watchful and if the crude methods of his emissaries had not awakened these independent republics to the danger they were running if they were to let him have his way. Even so, that propaganda continues, morning, noon, and night, and is as much of a menace to our own prestige as before.

19. He wanted to isolate Russia. Russia has been isolated.

20. He wanted to impress Finland with the desirability of a union with Germany to offset the danger which threatens that republic from the side of the Soviets. So far, he seems to have been quite successful in his negotiations, but they have not yet been finished and so we cannot yet tell what will happen.

21. He wanted to make every German in every part of

the world part of his shock troops in foreign lands and therefore preached the doctrine that the first allegiance of these immigrants is not to the country of their adoption but to the country of their birth. Even in this preposterous attempt to make people forget their oath of allegiance to the land that has given them hospitality, he has been much more successful than most of us seem to realize.

22. He has systematically endeavored to corrupt and to destroy that extremely useful code of international behavior which was known by the name of International Law. It had not yet reached the point of development at which it could really be regarded as Law, because there was no agency which could enforce the decisions of the different courts, such as the well-known Tribunal of The Hague. At the same time it was being more and more respected and was beginning to give the world at large the prospect of a society in which Reason would be substituted for Violence. Today, International Law no longer exists. The jungle law of the gangster has taken its place, and that this has happened is the result of the activities of Adolf Hitler.

23. He has systematically tried to corrupt the moral point of view of youth in every part of the world by appealing to that instinct of rowdyism which lies dormant in every child and which has to be overcome by years of a most careful sort of training. He has not only tried to do so but he has been completely successful in his own country, and he is now also beginning to be increasingly successful in most of the adjoining countries, for every boy loves to swagger around with a dagger and a sneer, and Hitler has provided him with a definite philosophy of life with which to bolster up his pretensions.

24. He has attacked that formidable Citadel of Scholarship which during the last four hundred years had been most carefully built up by the best elements in German society. He realized that an independent form of scholarship would be a menace to the irresponsible pseudo science which he needed to keep alive those racial hatreds which form such an important subject on the Nazi program of social destruction. Today, independent German scholarship no longer exists. It has been destroyed by Adolf Hitler.

25. He has filled the world with a sense of terror it had seldom experienced before. He has turned servant against master and master against servant, and son against father and father against son, and wife against husband and husband against wife, that by a mutual feeling of suspicion and distrust all of them might fall victims to that unreasoning dread of the unexpected which is the very core of the philosophy of terror.

26. He has done his best to substitute the ideal of the mucker for that of the gentleman, and few phases of his pernicious propaganda have met with such unanimous success as this one. Which need not surprise us, as it relieves (temporarily at least) the creature of inferior qualities from that almost insufferable consciousness of his own low status which has always made him the most dangerous enemy of a truly cultured state of society.

27. He has set out to deprive society of the only basis upon which it could ever hope to establish a truly civilized and lasting form of international co-operation. He denounced the Sermon on the Mount as maudlin ravings on the part of an itinerant Jewish carpenter. For this I shall not judge him. I shall leave him to the mercies of Almighty God.

A nice little list this, especially the political end of it! Just a few modest desires on the part of a poor, hardworking nation which did not get a square deal. Sixty million people living within a territory not quite as large as Texas but deprived by their wicked neighbors of every opportunity to lead a normal existence, to acquire colonies, to share the warm rays of that sun which shines so beautifully upon the slums of Marseilles and the tenements of Glasgow. One feels inclined to inquire why, unlike Sweden, Norway, Switzerland, unlike all the most enlightened nations in this world, Germany and Italy must put pressure campaigns upon all mothers and must use every possible method for an artificial increase in the total volume of its cannon fodder, so that a hundred people are forced to get sustenance from those vegetable gardens and grain fields which could easily feed ten but can never hope to support a hundred, let alone a thousand.

And there is of course that pathetic story which has been so often repeated that now all the subjects of the Third Reich firmly believe it—the fable about the poor Germans who had all their wealth stolen by the greedy Allies and who thereupon had to start again from scratch and that in a country, that had practically no raw materials. I hold no brief for the Allies. The Treaty of Versailles was both cruel and unjust. But how about the hundreds—yes, the thousands of millions of dollars and crowns and guilders and pounds that were poured into Germany after the war by way of municipal and state loans and private loans so that the Germans could rebuild their hospitals and their lodginghouses and their ports and their railroad stations and roads and could construct their *Bremens* and *Europas* and all those other magnificent older liners with which for years they beat the Allied steamship companies at their own game?

We are all of us only too familiar with this sad chapter of deliberate deceit. We know that not a cent of this money was returned or ever will be returned, that not a penny of interest on these loans was ever paid or ever will be paid. But it makes a good propaganda story with which to keep the Germans in a perpetual state of resentment at their sad fate and to make them feel that now they have a perfect right to despoil their neighbors far and wide and to grab everything in sight, because they had been cheated out of their birthright as one of the leading nations of the world.

But these facts are only too well known to all of us. No need to dwell upon them here. For in this little book I am mainly concerned with the question: Why must we prepare to defend ourselves against the aggressions of the man who has so cleverly capitalized upon the grievances (imaginary and otherwise) of his followers that the whole of our planet is gradually being turned into one vast armed camp which absorbs the money that should really be used for an entirely different purpose—for the purpose of reshaping our modern world into a place that shall be really fit for decent human habitation?

I tried to paint you a picture of the man responsible for this reign of spiritual and physical terror. And in trying to be fair to him, I almost bent backwards to give him the benefit of every possible scrap of doubt. Whether I have succeeded in doing this, I do not know. For I can hear the reader say, "But all you told us so far about Adolf Hitler reads like a Horatio Alger story, *From Rags to Riches*—the small-town boy who made good in the big city." Or words to that effect.

Undoubtedly if that had been all there was to this Tale of Two Countries, we could only applaud his achievements, for surely over here in America we admire the fellow who has struggled up from poverty—who overcame all his original handicaps and who from a plain private soldier became commander-in-chief of all the armies of the most powerful state since the days of Napoleon.

But that is not all there is to it, not by any manner of means. For our native success story, in order to be truly appreciated, must lead up to a final apotheosis in which all these great achievements are being used for the ultimate benefit of mankind. When they serve a contrary purpose, we denounce the so-called hero and hate him as ever since the beginning of time we have abhorred that god who could use his powers only for purposes of evil and who became a devil.

It looked as if the idea of a personal Devil, that strange reincarnation of all that was ignoble and merciless and mean, had left us with the Dark Ages. But now, after almost four centuries, he is once more back among us. The historian and the physician may explain the career of Hitler upon purely scientific grounds. The average man, who follows his instincts in such matters and who quite often is nearer to the truth than the professor, will reach back to the Devil of his ancestors to find an answer to the perplexing question: How could one single person do quite so much mischief and that in quite such a short space of time?

I am afraid that he will never receive a satisfactory answer. But meanwhile, he will have to realize that this Power of Evil has returned to our world and that it is greedily reaching out towards our own shores and that we cannot possibly hope to safeguard ourselves from its contaminating touch by an appeal to reason, since reason is now denounced by all faithful Nazis as merely an outworn form of Jewish logic.

Nor can we expect to do any better with paper treaties, since they are not worth the parchment on which they stand engraved. Nor by solemn agreements, which are never meant to be kept. Nor by any of those agreements against sudden aggression, which are without value when they come from a man to whom the sacredness of an oath seems to mean as little as a pledge of loyalty to a friend. It is a dreadful choice which we shall be called upon to make during the next two or three months. Do we want to follow the example of Great Britain and surrender abjectly to the blackmail of a gunman, or shall we face the facts in all their stark brutality and hasten to protect our country by such terrific barriers of warships and airplanes that not even a madman, in his most irresponsible moments, would dare to risk an attack? There is only one answer and all of us know it!

Bismarck, fighting with his back against the wall and referring to one of the most humiliating episodes in the history of Germany during the Middle Ages, coined the proud phrase: "We do not intend to go to Canossa."

I offer a modern version of that historic utterance and speaking for the whole of our people, I promise Adolf Hitler this:

"We will never come to Berchtesgaden."

There was a time and a day when one of the most intelligent among those who gave us our independence thought that the moment had come to explain unto the other nations of this earth those principles upon which the rebels across the Atlantic intended to found an independent commonwealth of their own. And if I remember rightly, he spoke as follows:

"We hold these truths to be self-evident; that all men are created equal, that they are endowed by their Creator with certain inalienable Rights, and that among these are Life, Liberty and the pursuit of Happiness."

That was the spiritual philosophy of our American Democracy a century and a half ago. It still is today.

Whenever Goebbels and his henchmen get hold of such a declaration of faith as I have just written down, they immediately delve deep into their archives and in that particular literary jargon which they have affected since their rise to power and which bears about the same relation to first-rate German prose as the Austrian-Teutonic dialect of the Führer (with its harsh

Czechish intonations) bears to the language as spoken by a cultivated person from Lübeck or Vienna, they will favor us with a lengthy enumeration of all the many times when we ourselves have failed most shamefully to live up to the high promises of our immortal Declaration of Independence.

No one can deny that we have done so upon a great many—yea, upon far too many occasions. Just as no one can accuse me of an exaggerated and one-sided patriotism if I claim that whenever we were unfaithful to the best of our traditions there invariably arose a mighty leader whose voice promptly called us back to a realization of our duties and bade us remember that we, blessed among all the nations of this earth by the riches of our heritage, have been put under a most solemn obligation to act as guardians and protectors of the noblest words ever writ into a document of state, those simple words which guaranteed unto every man the right to be the master of his own fate and to decide for himself how and in what manner he will endeavor to achieve his own ideal of happiness.

We are a curious people. Just now we are slowly preparing to elect someone to act as our leader during the coming years. For of course, we too have our Führer. The difference is that we, over here, elect him of our own free will, but with the understanding that we can get rid of him again in case we find that he does not come up to our expectations. But being a young nation and quite boisterous in everything we do, we love this sort of rough-and-ready combat that goes by the name of an "American election," and we enter into the fray as if it were a matter of life and death and as if at any moment we might pull out our pistols and bowie knives and go after each other like cowboys in the prehistoric days of the frontier, fighting for a water hole.

But let there be no mistake about our real underlying feelings. We may disagree with all our politicians, we may even denounce our Chief Executive as a traitor to his country. We may even grow very sarcastic about the ability of the average citizen to take care of himself, but let us suspect the slightest threat to our Democracy, to our good right to manage our own affairs as we ourselves see fit, and suddenly it will be discovered that all of us see eye to eye, from Franklin Delano Roosevelt to Herbert Hoover, from the most convinced Democrat to the bitterest of Republicans, and that each and every one of us is ready to forget his personal differences and rush to the defense of that which we consider our highest good—our totally irrational and completely preposterous and our eternally beloved Democracy.

That I think is about all I had to say and so I had better stop talking. But I hope that I have made myself entirely clear. There can be no compromise between our own ideas concerning the Good Life and those of Adolf Hitler. There can be no spiritual peace between the citizens of the United States of America and the subjects of the Führer of the Third Reich. There can only be war until one of us or the other suffers defeat.

About the outcome of this conflict, none of us can have the slightest doubt.

For in the truest sense of the word, it will be our battle, since we shall fight it for the proud maintenance of those ideals and principles which alone can give meaning to the lives of the sort of people we ourselves happen to be.

May the spirit of Washington, Jefferson and Abraham Lincoln guide our steps and enlighten us in our choice, for upon our decision rests the fate of the world to come.

10.20 P.M., OCTOBER 21, 1938.

For further details see your daily newspapers!

A NOTE ABOUT THE AUTHOR

HENDRIK WILLEM VAN LOON is of Dutch stock. So far as he has ever been able to discover, all his ancestors until the beginning of the sixteenth century were Dutch, with the exception of his maternal grandfather, who came from the German duchy of Oldenburg. All his ancestors were Protestant, except one of his grandmother's uncles, who became a Roman Catholic, and who, after a great deal of wandering across the Balkans, died Archbishop of Constantinople. The author was brought up in Holland until his twentieth year, when he came to his ancestral estates on the banks of the Hudson. He spent several years with the Associated Press. During the Russian revolution of 1906, he was sent for two months to St. Petersburg, where he took the place of the regular correspondent who was on a short leave of absence. Since then—the summer of 1906—he has spent a great deal of his time in Germany. He stayed for five years in Munich, where he took his Ph.D. Afterwards he used to visit Germany until the Nazis came to power. As he has steadily warned America against the Nazi peril (both in writing and over the radio), he could not go to Germany, but he spent four months this summer in those countries which are geographically closest to Germany, and where he could get as much firsthand information as possible about the situation in the Reich. He returned to America early in October. This book is the result of a voyage of discovery which filled him with fear for the future of our own country—unless we realize, here and now, the menace of a political philosophy which is the sworn enemy of every form of democracy.